BONN

M

Personal glimpses into the lives of
thirty missionary ladies

SARAH

AND HER MISSIONARY
DAUGHTERS

Sarah and Her Missionary Daughters

by Bonnie Markham

©Copyright 1998 Word Aflame Press
Hazelwood, MO 63042-2299

Cover Design by Paul Povolni

Printed in the United States of America

Printed by

WORD AFLAME®PRESS
8855 DUNN ROAD
HAZELWOOD, MO 63042-2299

Library of Congress Cataloging-in-Publication Data

Markham, Bonnie Jean, 1942-
Sarah and her missionary daughters: personal glimpses into the lives of thirty missionary ladies / by Bonnie Markham
    p. cm.
ISBN 1-56722-210-2
1. Women missionaries—United States—Biography. 2. Pentecostal churches—Missions—History. I. Title.
BV2565.M37 1998
266' .994'0922—dc21   97-50221
   [B]   CIP

In loving memory
of a great lady

Audrene Hruza Scism

missionary to India, gentle,
quiet, obedient to her husband,
even as Sarah

"Whose adorning . . . let it be . . . the ornament of a meek and quiet spirit . . . even as Sarah."

"Sarah obeyed Abraham."

"Sarah, . . . whose daughters ye are."

"Whose daughters ye are, as long as ye do well."

"Whose daughters ye are . . . as long as ye . . . are not afraid."

(See I Peter 3:3-6.)

Contents

Foreword

by Robert Trapani

Sarah and Her Missionary Daughters focuses on why, of all the Old Testament women, Sarah is the only one God mentions as our model in home and marriage. Bonnie Markham has endeavored to examine the battle-grounds and the tools of victory in being a Christian woman in today's world. Abraham may be the father of faith, but Sarah is the mother of the fearless!

A woman's perspective on the unfairness of life situations reveals that "Life is not fair, but God is just." There is One who knows what we can bear and promises never to put upon us more than we can bear. There will come the day of recognition when our Lord will reward those who walked not just by feelings but without fear by holding on to the promises of God.

Sarah, who lived with great disappointments and pains in her life, is the only example that the New Testament gives for how a wife ought to be. She was strong, powerful, decisive. She was capable of deep feelings and frustrations, and yet she had a courage that certainly marked her in God's hall of fame.

When we speak of Abraham as the father of faith, we should not overlook the lady who was the mother of the nonfearing. The vicissitudes of her marriage are as powerful a story as anything today. Married to a great man of God, as history now declares, her character perhaps contributed greatly to making Abraham the father of faith. He was a man who could storm across the desert in pursuit of five kings who had sacked Sodom and stolen his nephew and family. Sarah lived with a warrior. Yet this was a man who not once, but twice, denied Sarah as wife, calling her "sister," to protect himself in his fear. Twice she was taken from him to be another man's wife or part of his harem, and only God rescued her from the situation each time. At this point in his life, the man of faith was overcome by fear.

Sarah was a woman who loved her man so much that she made as great a sacrifice as any woman could. In her efforts to help him receive the promise of God, the vision of sons and family, she gave her own handmaiden to bear him the child that she could not. What were her thoughts? A man who had taken no other wives or concubine was asked to raise up a child through another woman. She saw his weaknesses of character, but her commitment was not to walk in fear but in the promise of God.

Today many Christian women face battles that are every bit as devastating as those fought by Abraham on the plain outside of Sodom. Attacks come from without and within. Outside attacks come from expectations of what she is to be. It is so difficult to be measured by the scale of a changing society and a last days' world that is "without natural affection." A world that ridicules submissiveness as a dirty word and honoring husband as something out of a generation read about only in old novels. This is a time when crushing pressures distort the unique individuality of a woman, by pressures to conform to the current fads and fashions.

The pressures from within may well be even greater. How can we measure the emotional scarring from the past? The voices of yesteryear that degrade a woman and deny her right to be something of worth? She must learn to deal with the scars of childhood, the wounds of young womanhood, the bruises of adjustments to marriage, and sharing a life, values, and direction with another person.

These are things that cause many a woman to wish to collapse, perhaps to escape, to be free from never-ending constraints.

Daughters of Sarah understand fear, but they refuse to be driven by fear. They do not deny frightening situations but instead refuse to let their lives be devastated by them.

Sarah and Her Missionary Daughters promises to be a much-needed examination of the power of the woman who trusts the Lord.

God, give to us daughters of Sarah! Women who have learned the unchanging principles of God and are not afraid to march boldly into this closing generation!

Robert Trapani is pastor of the United Pentecostal Church in Akron, Ohio. He had a counseling office in Akron for ten years and is a member of the American Association of Christian Counselors. He travels extensively all over the world, ministering and counseling individuals and families in crisis.

Acknowledgments

My undying thanks to each lady who
took time from her busy schedule to
write, often painfully, her portion
of this book. God bless each of you in
Jesus' name.

Thanks to Joan Howard, Jeannie
Steward, and Michael Martin
for the many hours of help.

A particular tribute to my daughter,
Tracie Markham,
for her willingness to be actively
involved in our missionary work.
She willingly shared the heights
and endured the depths of life on
the foreign field. More than a daughter,
she has proved to be my co-worker
and very faithful friend.

Introduction

The purpose of this book is to help the many ladies who feel the Lord is calling them to do something for Him. Some are hindered by feelings of unworthiness; some fear that they are incapable of doing what He is asking. Every normal person has fears and self-doubts. However, to be a daughter of Sarah we must not allow those fears to stop us from serving the Lord in whatever capacity He asks. Sometimes it will be to play the piano in church in spite of fear of criticism, to witness to a neighbor, or to go to the foreign field.

The following ladies have their share of faults and fears to overcome; if perfection were necessary, there would be no missionaries. Their stories are not to tell what they have accomplished on the field but their lives *before* they went to the field. It is to show that God calls a wide variety of normal women from normal and abnormal backgrounds to work for Him. Please notice the vast differences in personalities, backgrounds, and experiences among these women. Some of them were reared in pastors' homes; others were from severely dysfunctional families. One missionary lady, who could not bring herself to write of her childhood, was severely beaten almost daily by parents who were thought to be true Christians. She had to struggle with believing God loved her while being mistreated at home. She won the battle and realized others had chosen to disobey God. He was not responsible nor was she, and God would deal with the guilty. Their evil was no excuse for immorality on her part. Victory did not come overnight but she overcame evil with good and is now able to help others who have suffered the same. Although some were not reared in a Christian home, they always had a desire to serve the Lord; others didn't have the slightest intention of serving God—much less being a missionary! A few determined to marry a minister; others were equally determined *not* to marry a preacher. Several were anxious to serve God on a foreign field, but many strongly fought against going. Some had difficulty leaving personal possessions for various reasons; a few had no problem leaving all, while others had nothing to leave. Many had a personal call from God; the Lord never dealt with many personally, but they had faith in their husband's call. A few attended Bible Schools; most did not. The Board appointed some the first time they met them; others had to meet them often. What a variety! Only a minority lost a loved one, though they all accepted that fearful risk when they put God first in their life. Some have been on the field many years, others for less time. Women have gone to the field as a single, as newlyweds, mothers of young babies or toddlers and, more rarely, teenagers. Some even went after they were grandmothers, including a widowed grandmother. The only thing they all have in common is an intense desire to please the Lord and the willingness to work extremely hard in His service.

Some have written more than others, but the length in no way shows the significance of their contribution to the work of God. Heaven alone will reveal their achievements. Each is responsible only for her own portion of the book.

Many other missionary ladies are continuing to do all they can for the Lord. Unfortunately, all could not be included. Every woman who is loyal to God and does not allow fear to hinder her work for Him, is a daughter of Sarah. Each daughter is a precious jewel in the royal diadem created to crown His Majesty, the Lord Jesus Christ,

Father of us all.

Just as I stand in awe of Sarah, I also absolutely marvel at her daughters at home and abroad. God bless you in His incomparable name as you become acquainted with a few daughters of Sarah.

CHAPTER 1

Sarah

by Bonnie Markham

"Dear God, I would rather die than live through this!" In the darkness Sarai shuddered and pulled her shawl tightly around her shoulders. Her long, dark hair was loose, and stray strands shifted with her movements. Her dress skimmed the sand as she restlessly walked away from her tent and farther from the camp. It wasn't the chilly breeze that made her shiver; it was raw, tormented emotions. Shame caused her cheeks to burn, and the wrenching pain in her heart produced an unending flow of tears.

In the bright but moonless night, the sky seemed almost overcrowded with stars, each one sharp and distinct, a vivid reminder of her failure to conceive the promised seed. She knew guards were posted around the caravan and always felt safe in her frequent evening walks away from the camp. Tonight, however, she felt that she would prefer to die than to stay inside her tent. As she nervously walked about, she forced her mind to concentrate on why and how this all began. She couldn't bear to think that at this moment her beloved husband, Abram, was in the arms of her Egyptian handmaiden, Hagar!

She could still picture her home in Mesopotamia, the great city of Ur with its beautiful streets, fountains, and great libraries. She recalled being surrounded by friends and family. Oh, how she had loved her comfortable home and the joy brought to it by the mere presence of Abram and her love for him! The only thing missing had been the child, for which she so desperately longed. With each passing year it had become more difficult to respond politely to the rude, probing remarks about her childlessness. Abram's love for her had made the distress and reproach of being childless easier to bear, although she knew he also yearned for a child.

A short distance away, she heard the voice of a man caring for his camels, and it drew her mind back to the present, reviving the stabbing pain in her breast. She compelled herself to think of the night Abram first told her they would be leaving Ur.

The news had come as a shock, and questions had tumbled from her lips: "What? Why? Where are we going?" She might have thought he was teasing had it not been for the seriousness of his expression. Abram answered all that he knew: "God spoke to me and said, 'Get out of your country and from your kindred, and come into the land that I shall show you.'" Her mind had whirled in confusion and unasked questions had rushed through her thoughts: When did He tell you this? Was it a vision? A dream? An audible voice? She knew he would eventually tell her these things, but at the moment she was overwhelmed with reality. The painful fact remained that she would soon be leaving her home and beloved family.

Abram had sighed deeply as though a great weight

had been lifted from him. After telling her, he rolled over and was soon in a sound sleep. Sarai had stayed awake for hours. She had learned long ago to be submissive to her husband; nevertheless, the magnitude of his words penetrated deep within her being, the effect nearly paralyzing. She labored in travail many nights before giving birth to the faith that led her to accept God's will. Even though it had been extremely difficult, she had begun preparing for the move.

Sitting down and pushing her sandal-clad feet deep into the cooling sand, she let her mind wander back to the turmoil and confusion of their last days in Ur. They had packed some things to take with them, sold what they couldn't take, and given many articles to friends and loved ones. Oh, the questions people had asked, Sarai recalled, and their laughter when she and Abram had answered, "Our God has called. We must go and trust Him to lead us."

Tonight she sat brooding on the memories that seemed to flow past her eyes as she recalled leaving all her loved ones. She had felt that her heart would break, knowing she would probably never see them again. After their departure, she cried off and on for days but determinedly refused to look back or consider returning to her own country. Instead, she resolutely followed her husband. What a caravan that had been as they left Ur and traveled to Haran: hundreds of sheep, camels, cattle, tents, household supplies, and servants!

Letting the sand sift through her fingers, she reflected back to the time when Abram had been seventy-five years old and she sixty-five. They had departed from Haran after the death of his father, Terah. By then, they had acquired an even larger host of servants and possessions.

It had been frightening to leave Ur, and she was apprehensive again as they left Haran. It was not uncommon for even large caravans to be attacked by marauding bands from numerous tribes and nations; however, she had determined within herself to trust the Lord to care for them.

Soon after they left Haran and reached the plain of Moreh, the Lord appeared to Abram again, saying, "Unto your seed I will give this land," and Abram built an altar to Him there. Sarai had been thrilled to hear of the promised seed. Surely this must mean that I will have a child soon! she had thought joyfully.

Customarily, men had a number of wives and concubines; however, Abram had never considered taking another woman because of his deep love for Sarai. It had always been a great comfort to her, even though it left him childless, to have a husband who loved her so much that he would refuse to take another woman. She had been convinced that God would soon open her barren womb and she would present Abram with a son.

She remembered how happily she had left the plain of Moreh after the promise from God. They had traveled to Bethel, where Abram again built an altar and called on the name of the Lord. Soon after, they journeyed south and encountered such a severe famine that she wondered, Have we missed the will of God? Would He call us to a country so *unfruitful*? The barren country around them had forced them to go into Egypt.

The thought of the word *barren* jarred her back to the present, causing her to think of Abram now lying with the other woman. "I can't endure this," she wept. "I love him! I don't want him with her!" She rose quickly to her feet and walked even farther from the camp, pulling her heavy shawl up to cover her head as the night became more chilly. She felt as if time had dug its heels into the sand and refused to budge. Would this night never end? "Oh, why must this be, Lord? Why couldn't *I* have had his child? Why?"

Remembering the famine that forced them to continue into Egypt also brought memories of when Abram, to ensure his own protection, had asked her to say that she was merely his sister. It was a risk, for everyone in the caravan knew they were married. They could have told Pharaoh! Nevertheless, Abram felt it was a risk worth taking, for he was sure that Sarai was such a beautiful woman that Pharaoh would have been willing to kill her husband in order to have her for his wife.

It hurt to see Abram receiving sheep, oxen, male servants, and especially *female* servants in exchange for her. He believes God will take care of me, but why doesn't he believe Him for his own protection? she wondered. "Besides, I'm sure Pharaoh wouldn't have wanted me had he known my age and how long I had been married."

What *had* the people in the caravan thought of the lies? "But You were merciful to me, Lord, and for my sake plagued Pharaoh and his house, causing him to return me to Abram. Thank You, Lord. For even though I get weary of the constant moving around, the wind, the sand, the famines, the quarrels among the people, and the frightening unknown, I would rather remain with Abram as a pilgrim until we reach the land You promised than to stay in Pharaoh's palace, enjoying the comforts and pleasures for a season."

Persisting in this train of thought, her mind's eye envisioned them as they left Egypt and returned to Bethel, the place of the altar.

By then the quarrels among the people had become so sharp that a split became inevitable. Abram had given Lot and his herdsmen the first choice of the land. Lot had chosen the gardenlike plain of Jordan, but he later moved into the city of Sodom. Sarai wondered why Abram had offered Lot first choice, when Abram rightfully should have chosen first. In fact, she wondered why Abram had allowed Lot to accompany them since the Lord had told Abram to leave his kindred. But the Lord had blessed Abram and had promised him all the land as far as he could see, from the east, west, north, and south, and had extended the promise to his seed forever, who would become as numerous as the dust of the earth. There it was again! Another promise from God that Abram would be a father. Oh, surely now I shall bear a child, Sarai had believed.

Time moved on, but Sarai had remained childless.

One night Sarai had nearly been frightened to death when a messenger arrived, yelling and babbling as he called for Abram to come quickly. The messenger was breathless; his panic hardly allowed him to deliver his story. In a fear-filled voice, he managed to tell Abram about the attack on the city of Sodom and of his own terrifying escape. He told him that four kings with a host of soldiers had terrorized much of the country while slaughtering other kings and nations. The kings of Sodom and Gomorrah joined three other kings and met the enemy in the valley of Siddim, where a horrendous battle had taken place. The kings of Sodom and Gomorrah had been defeated. Sodom was immediately overrun by the enemy; Lot and many others had been taken prisoners.

Sarai had nearly panicked as Abram began shouting orders to his men. Within moments, they grabbed their weapons, and the whole caravan became an uproar of preparations for battle.

"Abram, don't leave!" Sarai had pleaded. "What if they attack us while you are gone? Please, Abram, stay here!"

"Sarai, it would be better to fight them away from the camp, and fight them we must. I'm counting on you to help restore order here as soon as possible. I'll leave some men on watch, but I must go!" In a flurry of action, dust, and shouts, he was gone. In spite of her fear, she knew she must keep her wits about her if she was to be of any help to anyone. This thought plunged her into the unexpected activities she knew had to be done. How fervently she had prayed for the men's safe and quick return. She also feared that those remaining at camp would be attacked!

Abram had taken 318 of his own armed and trained men, along with some Amorites with whom he was confederate, to battle. After much savage fighting, they defeated the enemy in the valley of Shaveh and rescued Lot and many others. Abram's safe return left Sarai thrilled and vastly relieved.

"Abram is a mighty man of God," Sarai now whispered aloud. Looking up once more to the innumerable stars, she remembered that after this battle to rescue Lot the Lord had brought Abram forth to look at the stars and said, "So shall your seed be." Abram believed in the Lord, and He had counted it to him for righteousness.

"Lord, I believed I would bear the child, being Abram's only woman. Some men even divorce their wives after discovering their barren condition, but Abram has repeatedly reassured me that he would never leave nor forsake me. I've had visual reminders of Your promise all around me: the dust by day and the stars by night." As she spoke, she felt as though someone tenderly brushed her cheek; she sensed a Presence in the silence.

"But how long could I ask Abram to wait? We have been married for so long and have been in Canaan ten years, and I am still barren. Forgive my past selfishness, Lord, in hindering Abram from having a child by another woman." She stopped, allowing her entire being to absorb the sight of the thousands of stars shining in the heavens above. Her shattered soul cried out, "O God, why am I unfruitful? Why can't I be the mother of my beloved husband's descendants? I want so much to be a help and a blessing to him—why am I like this? I know that I am now seventy-five years old, but surely nothing is too hard for You!" Then after a moment she added, "You never said *I* would be a mother. You said only that Abram would be a father. For all these years I have resisted sharing him because I love him. Besides, it just doesn't seem right! But I am so weary, Lord. I am tired of the struggle to uphold my confidence that I will bear the child, especially when time and facts seem to scoff at my convictions, not to mention all the people."

Continuing to walk across the sand, she recalled her months of struggling with an idea before she finally surrendered her dreams and suggested to Abram that he have a child by a substitute woman. She had carefully considered the many young servant girls in the caravan and had decided on Hagar, even though she was an Egyptian. She and Sarai had gotten along well since she had selected Hagar to be her personal handmaiden. Sarai was sure Hagar would produce a fine, healthy son for Abram. After all these years, Sarai decided she must abandon her own desires and dignity and stop hindering what she by now assumed to be the will of God.

One night, after everyone had retired, she turned to Abram, determined to control her tears, and said, "The Lord has restrained me from bearing. Please, go in to my maid; it may be that I will obtain children by her." To confess my failure to conceive, thus accepting this great reproach, is humiliating, she had thought. To admit, even now, that I am barren is devastating, but I am seventy-five and he is eighty-five. How can I continue to deny it?

Abram had accepted her suggestion. Tonight he had gone in to Hagar. Now, Sarai was here alone, staring at the sand and stars—both reminders of her emptiness—alone, with a barren womb and a broken heart.

As the sky began to lighten in the east, Sarai walked slowly back to her tent. She was physically exhausted, and her mind felt as numb as her chilled body. As she reached for the tent flap, Abram stepped out. For a moment, they stood quiet and still, wordlessly looking into each other's eyes.

Abram tenderly reached out and brushed back the strands from her cheeks. "You frightened me, Sarai. When I returned hours ago you weren't here, and I . . . I . . . I love you, Sarai."

She hadn't known how she would react at this encounter. Leaning her head onto his chest, she began to sob as he placed his strong arms around her murmuring, "Sarai, Sarai, my darling Sarai."

It was with mixed emotions that Sarai learned of Hagar's conception. It was so quick! Sarai had hoped so very much to bear the child herself, but at least Abram would now be a father. To spare Sarai's feelings, Abram continued to reaffirm his love for her and refrained from giving Hagar any special attention. Sarai, however, was careful to be considerate of her handmaiden's condition, making everything as easy as possible for Hagar.

Sarai was surprised to notice Hagar's change of attitude after she conceived. Not only did she take advantage of Sarai's consideration toward her, but she began behaving with insolence and haughtiness. Sarai continued to treat her kindly and even had other servants perform Hagar's more difficult duties. It wasn't long before the other servants carefully let Sarai know of the critical things Hagar had been saying about her. One even quoted an old proverb, "There are four things the earth cannot bear, and one of them is a handmaid that is heir to her mistress." Sarai, however, was a gentle lady with a kind spirit and continued making allowances for Hagar's behavior, although it was becoming increasingly more difficult.

One evening Sarai asked Hagar to do a simple task. Hagar whirled on her and replied, "Do it yourself! You're no better than anyone else." Sarai was speechless for a moment. In a fury she turned and dashed from the tent in search of Abram. Trembling with rage, she found him and said, "My wrong be upon you! I gave my maid into your embrace; and when she saw that she had conceived, *I* became despised in *her* eyes. The Lord judge between you and me."

Abram simply replied, "She is your maid; correct her."

Sarai marched back to the tent as she thought, What

a mistake I made, but the choice was his! She furiously informed Hagar, "Just because you are carrying Abram's child, you are in no way to think you can conduct yourself with such a contemptuous attitude. Neither I nor Abram will permit such despicable behavior. If you know what is good for you, you will comply with this warning!"

Hagar turned pale as she realized the serious mistake she had made in thinking she was now on Sarai's level. She regretted that she allowed how much she despised Sarai to be known. Without a word, she fled from the tent to escape Sarai's wrath.

It took Sarai some time to calm down as she was not accustomed to feeling or expressing such anger. When told that Hagar had fled into the wilderness alone, Sarai became worried and blamed herself. One moment she felt wrong for not being more tolerant of Hagar, and the next minute she felt her anger rising as she remembered Hagar's attitude. Her thoughts and feelings were a hot jumble of anger, self-justification, and self-blame. In spite of these emotions, Sarai was worried about Hagar alone in the wilderness, far from the protection of the camp.

Sarai's torment was short-lived, for Hagar soon returned and told Abram that God had met her by a fountain of water in the wilderness and told her to return and submit to Sarai. He had referred to Hagar as Sarai's maid and promised to make a multitude of people from the son she now carried, whom she was to name Ishmael.

Sarai noticed that although Hagar's behavior improved it was obvious that her feelings had not. The following months, as Hagar grew larger with child, were a torture to Sarai, and she deeply regretted her own error in suggesting that Abram take Hagar. She knew it was a mistake that she would deplore for the rest of her life. However, she determined to handle it as gracefully as she could.

Finally, the months of waiting were over, and once again Sarai sought solace in the silence of the desert

sands while the entire caravan became a scene of rejoicing and feasting. Hagar had given birth to Abram's son
Ishmael. At last Abram at age eighty-six was a father!
Looking back over the events of the day, Sarai knew she
had gone through all the appropriate motions of seeing
that Hagar had the best care available. She had even pre-
tended to be happy that Abram was a father, and in some
ways she was. At the same time, it hurt so much to know
that the child was not her own and would not suckle at
her own breasts. "Lord," she prayed as she walked alone,
"I have smiled today until I felt like my face would crack,
but You know it's been a phony smile. I feel like such a
hypocrite! O God, I have to have Your help. Please help
me to be kind to them. It's all my fault. Please don't let
me fail You again."

In spite of being pleased for Abram's sake that he at
last had a son, it remained an emotional trial for Sarai.
She saw the boy as he was nursed and cared for by
Hagar; she observed his first attempts to crawl, then to
walk, and eventually saw him darting in and out among
the tents. Often Abram would lift him up onto his camel,
where they would travel together as Abram taught him
many truths. He especially taught Ishmael about God, as
there were pagan Egyptians in the camp besides his
mother. Abram certainly didn't want his son to become
an idolater.

Time passed and Abram delighted in seeing the
growth and development of his son as he turned thirteen.
Abram was now ninety-nine. The Lord appeared to him
once again and told him that He was going to make an
everlasting covenant with him and his seed after him. God
changed his name from Abram to Abraham. "This is my
covenant, which you shall keep, between Me and you and
your seed after you: every male child among you shall be
circumcised." Then the Lord told Abraham, "As for Sarai
your wife, you shall not call her name Sarai, but Sarah
shall be her name. And I will bless her and also give you

a son by her; then I will bless her, and she shall be a mother of nations; kings of peoples shall be from her."

When Abraham heard this about Sarah, he fell on his face and laughed, saying in his heart, "Shall a child be born unto a man who is a hundred years old? And shall Sarah, who is ninety years old, bear a son? O that Ishmael might live before You!"

God replied, "Sarah your wife shall bear you a son indeed, and you shall call his name Isaac. I will establish My covenant with him for an everlasting covenant, and with his seed after him. And as for Ishmael, I have heard you. Behold, I have blessed him and will make him fruitful and will multiply him exceedingly. He shall beget twelve princes, and I will make him a great nation. But I will establish My covenant with Isaac, whom Sarah shall bear to you at this set time next year."

Shortly after, Jehovah and two angels appeared to Abraham as he sat in the door of his tent during the heat of the day. He bowed himself to the ground and offered to wash their feet and prepare them food. He then hastened to tell Sarah to make some bread while he made arrangements to have a calf prepared for them. After they had their feet washed and had eaten, the Lord asked about Sarah. Abraham told the Lord that she was in the tent. Actually she was very near the door and heard the Lord say, "I will certainly return to you according to the time of life, and behold, Sarah your wife shall have a son."

Sarah laughed within herself; this was just too much to accept after the endless years of disappointments. And at her age! The Lord then asked, "Why did Sarah laugh, saying, 'Shall I surely bear a child, since I am old?' Is anything too hard for the Lord?"

Frightened, Sarah denied laughing, but the Lord said, "No, but you did laugh." This time, however, He told her that she would be a mother. Her personal encounter with Him renewed her faith, and she believed.

Sarah had often taken walks at night when the air was

cool and she needed a quiet place to think or talk to the Lord. But one night that next year, as she walked, she began to count the stars and laugh, "One, two, three, four, five." Then she laughed again and pulled the covering back from her tiny son's face. "Look, Isaac, just look at all those stars! Six, seven, eight, nine, ten," she laughed again. "Truly they can't be counted. Oh, Isaac, what a great God we serve!"

She hugged him fiercely to her breast. Her love for him was like sheer bliss rising. Billowing higher and higher, it flowed through her like a consuming flood. "Isaac, I can't wait until you are old enough to understand. I will tell you now, and I'll tell you next year, and I'll tell you again and again till the day I die. My child, I am more than ninety years old. Ninety! Far too old to be holding my very first babe. When the Lord confirmed to us a year ago that you were to be born, your father and I both laughed because it was simply too good to be true. It has been over twenty-five years since you were promised, but now we are laughing from utter delight. God has made me to laugh, so all that hear will laugh with me, for I have borne Abraham a son in his old age. I may be over ninety, but I have never felt so young and lighthearted in all my life.

"I made a terrible mistake in getting ahead of God's plan, but He has proved that what He has promised He will bring to pass, even though we must sometimes wait many years. Now my little one, my little miracle, I have you; I will die before I let any harm come to you. See those stars, angel? So shall your descendants be, for you are the promised seed, and God has promised that He will establish His covenant with you. He promised you that, Isaac, He promised! And believe me, I know better than anyone that what God promised He *will* do!"

Standing alone in the darkness, Sarah became very still. As she held the cherished baby to her heart, she looked up into the endless expanse of stars and in her barest whisper prayed, "My Almighty God, I have come to this midnight altar to tell you again of my gratitude for the miracle I hold in my arms." As a holy hush surrounded her, she became unable to express the depth of her love for God and this child. The stars seemed close enough to gather with her fingertips. With profound reverence, she drank in the sight of the vast galaxies lighting her vision of the future. To think the Messiah would someday be born because she had cradled in her once-barren womb the one who symbolized the promise of His coming! More than giving birth to a child, she had given birth to a promise! Bowing her head in a prayer so deep it never escaped her lips, she added, "Lord, I know I am truly unworthy of this great honor, but I will do my *utmost* to love, nurture, and protect this son You have entrusted to me, the heir to your promises."

In a daze of fulfillment and utter contentment, Sarah suckled her son and cared for him day by day, her eyes delighting in the wonder of his quick growth and robust health. With great reluctance, she agreed that the time had come for Isaac to be weaned and began to plan the celebration feast of this great event. The entire caravan was invited. Abraham spared nothing; food and music were abundant. The people were delighted to see Abraham so happy and were thrilled to hear Sarah as she joyfully laughed and called to each one of them. Then, in the midst of all the joy and laughter, Sarah saw Ishmael, now a teenager, as he mocked and persecuted Isaac. She felt as if someone had thrown icy water on her. It was obvious that Ishmael shared his mother's resentment toward Isaac. Abraham must be informed of this.

Sarah waited until she and Abraham could be alone before telling him what she had witnessed. She reminded him, "God promised that Isaac was to be the heir of His promises and the son of the bondwoman shall not be heir with him. They must leave." It had grieved Abraham, but God told him not to be sorrowful because Sarah was correct. Abraham obeyed what the Lord had indicated and sent them away. God kept His promise concerning Ishmael and protected the young man and his mother in the wilderness when he heard the young man's voice. With deep regret Abraham later learned that in spite of her personal encounters with the Lord, Hagar chose to take a wife for Ishmael from the land of Egypt. Abraham would personally see to it that Isaac would take a bride from their own kindred.

Sarah and Abraham continued their nomadic life and lived in the land of the Philistines many days. At age 127 in Hebron, in the land of Canaan, Sarah died; Abraham mourned for Sarah and wept!

Genesis 3:20 calls Eve "the mother of all living." Mary was the mother of our Lord. Many wonderful women can be found on the pages of the Word of God. Nevertheless, if we do well and do not allow fear to hinder our walk with God, we are *Sarah's* daughters! (See I Peter 3:6.)

What an exalted position the Lord has given her! The only time the Old Testament spotlighted Sarah was during her most difficult hours, and the results of her error are still being felt today in the Middle East and around the world. Despite Sarah's well-known mistakes, she had many strong points. Sarah left all to follow her imperfect yet beloved husband, never returning to her own country. She was sixty-five years old when she left Haran, and she died at age 127, so she traveled sixty-two years!

Neither the desire to return to her home and country, nor the delights of Egypt and Pharaoh's palace, nor the dangers and difficulties of their journey deterred her from remaining a pilgrim in search of a city. Her husband told her that God had called him to a land that He would show him, but Abraham never found a permanent dwelling place for her. Wherever Abraham led, Sarah followed. Sometimes they stayed just a short time in one location; other times they stayed much longer. They were constantly moving from one field to the next, one country to another, encountering people of different languages, customs, food, and religions. There were many dangers resulting from the desert, heat, famines, and battles, as well as internal problems of a large caravan.

At the time of Lot's rescue, Abraham had 318 soldiers who had been born in his own house. To be the age of a soldier, they most likely had been born before they left Ur. If they were born "in his own house," Abraham was probably master of their parents as well. Besides the soldiers, there were wives, children, and other servants who took care of the many details necessitated by a caravan of this size. In Haran they acquired more possessions and servants, and they were given additional servants by the pharaoh in Egypt. No doubt their caravan grew to be an enormous mixed multitude. What a responsibility! We can only imagine the daily problems that must have demanded their attention. Many times it must have taken more courage, determination, and faith for Sarah to continue her journey those long sixty-two years than it did to leave the first time. What an awesome example for the wife of a pastor, evangelist, or missionary today!

When God made the covenant with Abraham, He changed Sarai's name to Sarah, which means princess. In spite of her error, she had proven herself in the eyes of God. In calling her His princess, He publicly placed His seal of approval on her.

When Sarah died, God's princess was given a most honorable burial. The only ground Abraham actually received in his lifetime was what he purchased at top price for Sarah's grave.

No one knows all of Sarah's thoughts, prayers, or deeds except for the Lord. Centuries after her death God moved on the apostle Peter to write her eulogy: A holy woman. Gentle. Quiet. Obedient to her husband.

Many good people have not answered the call to be a missionary because of feelings of inadequacy or a lack of understanding of how God works. They think, There is nothing special about me. My family background is not right. God never dealt with me, only my husband. My sinful life before God found me surely disqualifies me. Neither my husband nor I are superspiritual. My family is too close to bear separation.

Would Samuel have become the great prophet of Israel if Hannah had not been willing to give him up and leave him with Eli?

Would the son of the widow of Zarephath have survived if his mother had not sacrificed the last of his food to the man of God?

Would God have chosen Mary if her great spiritual experience would have caused her to usurp spiritual leadership and refuse to follow her husband, even into Egypt?

Would Ruth, a single, have become the bride of the "lord of the harvest" had she not been willing to leave her own country and to work in the field?

Rebekah left father and mother and went to a far country to meet her husband. It was in that distant land that she became the mother of thousands of millions after she entered into Sarah's tent.

These examples show that we can overcome all negative thoughts and accomplish the will of God. Because of Eve's disobedience to God, pain is associated with the birth of her children. Bondage is the heritage of Hagar's offspring. But the birth of Sarah's children is accompanied by laughter, joy, and freedom!

Like Sarah, all of the ladies in this book have experienced doubt as well as faith, defeat as well as victory, sickness as well as health. Some of them have followed their husbands from country to country. The Lord sent some to countries where they have enjoyed an abundance of spiritual rain; He sent others into places of severe spiritual famine. Most of these ladies are still on the mission field. A few went to the field intending to do their greatest work for Him there, but He wanted them to have field experience to equip them for the work He had for them in their home country.

I am convinced that God can use each of us, whether His plans for our lives include the foreign field or not. By reading about the deeds and emotions of these women we are able to identify with their feelings and realize that the Lord can make a beautiful vessel out of any humble clay that is yielded in His hands. Yes, these ladies are special, but then so are you. Every godly lady is a daughter of Sarah!

*Through faith also Sarah herself received strength to conceive seed, and was delivered of a child when she was past age, because **she** judged him faithful who had promised* (Hebrews 11:11).

Brother and Sister William Markham at the 1994 School of Missions.

Dinner in my house for all pastors and wives, 1986.

My daughter, Tracie, and I prepared all of the food for the construction crew at the building of our new church.

CHAPTER 2

Audrene Scism

INDIA

by Stan Scism

My mother was born in Rupert, Idaho, and given the name Gladys Audrene Hruza. Her father was Czech and her mother English. Because the name Gladys reminded her of a giggly, silly girl she knew, she always preferred to be called Audrene.

Both of her grandfathers farmed, but her father worked as an accountant and her mother taught school. Mother knew all about being a latchkey kid before that became newsworthy.

Although quiet and soft-spoken, she had a wonderful sense of humor and made my sister and me laugh by telling us stories of her youth. For example, one story described how the turkeys in her grandmother's orchard chased her. As a young lady at Bible college she smothered liver and onions with ketchup and bread before she could eat it. She thus taught us to be able to laugh at ourselves and to eat without complaint what our host set before us.

She loved God's Word, studied it, and taught us to do the same to prevent being misled by false messages and doctrines. During her teen years a message in tongues was given during a church service, followed by an interpretation along this line: "I am Jesus. I died on the cross for you. My body was broken for you. My bones were broken for you." Because of her knowledge of the Word, she recognized immediately that the message was false because the Bible says Jesus' bones were *not* broken.

After high school graduation, she worked for a year in an office; then she went to Bible college at Pentecostal Bible Institute for two years. During her last year, she studied in Portland, Oregon, at Conquerors Bible College, where she met Harry Scism. They had been childhood sweethearts when Harry's father, Ellis, had pastored in Rupert, before taking his family to India. By the spring semester, Audrene and Harry were dating. That summer, they were married. Dad worked fast!

Because my grandfather had become a missionary to India, that is where my father spent his teen years. When he and Mom married, she knew she would become a missionary there also, although as a child she had thought she would someday be a missionary to China.

She studied Hindustani and soon spoke it better than her missionary husband. She helped him found a church in central India, which led to the entire Central Indian and North Indian United Pentecostal Church fellowships. She was willing to adjust to rugged living conditions, prepare for shortages, and laugh when awkwardness became absurd.

Along with my father, she taught most of the Northeast Indian church leadership, who proclaimed her the best of the Bible teachers and who now lead seventy thousand saints.

When my sister and I were small, she opened to us the

love of books and learning, and would read as long as we would listen. When my father was the regional field supervisor over Asia and the South Pacific, he would have to be gone for long stretches of time. During these times she worked to help bring me out of my introversion. She engaged in innumerable bedside lectures that, even though I tired of them then, have had lasting benefit. She held the family together through years of difficulty and strains caused by church work. She gave and gave and gave to demand after demand, sacrificing herself over and over for the Lord, her family, and the work of God.

She prayed. Many times as children we came to her for help to find her on her knees. Many times she gave advice straight from that time of prayer.

During her years as wife of the director of the Foreign Missions Division at headquarters in Missouri, she helped her two teenagers in their struggles to understand and cope with their new lives in America. Both the American church culture and the culture of American society were new and strange to us.

Her intelligence won deep respect from her children. She advised with wisdom, and we both did our best to benefit from her counsel. If we are able to breathe fresh air into other people's lives, it is because the wind of the Spirit blew from her life into ours.

Was she perfect? No. She worried too much and was timid to a fault. Because she loved to laugh, she would not object to the following observation: In the family's Winnie the Pooh cycle, she was Piglet to her daughter's Winnie; I was Owl; Dad, Tigger; and Grandfather Scism, Eeyore.

Because of her gentle godliness, courage, and strength, she deserved, and received, the undying love of many people.

I, for one, miss her. I miss her a lot.

Audrene Scism with ladies in Northeast India.

Audrene Scism with children in Bombay, India

Audrene Scism with Mother Teresa in Calcutta, India

Audrene Scism with Ellis Scism and one of the oldest United Pentecostal Church ministers of Northeast India.

CHAPTER 3

Patricia Burgess

ARGENTINA, PARAGUAY, AND URUGUAY

My mother and father were married in an Assemblies of God church in Avondale, Arizona. My father had just returned from World War II. He was reared Baptist and had promised the Lord that if He would spare his life he would join the church when he got home. Before they were married, my mother had received the Holy Ghost and was baptized in Jesus' name.

My dad was under conviction and decided to move to California. Soon after they arrived in Shafter, California, Cletus Floyd baptized him in Jesus' name, and he received the Holy Ghost. Five months after I was born in Wasco, California, they moved back to Avondale. I was taught to love the Lord and trust him for everything. Church was always the most important thing in our lives. I can remember six-week revivals, with services every night; we never missed a service—even on school nights.

My folks, Elmer and Lucille Compton, started the church in Avondale, Arizona, when I was nine years old. Our little group couldn't find a pastor, so my mother became a licensed minister and pastored until they could get a man to take the church. She knocked doors every Saturday and was insistent that I accompany her. One of the doors was answered by a lady who is still in the Avondale church today. I really thank the Lord for a godly, faithful mom and dad. They have given me a beautiful Pentecostal heritage.

I was baptized in an irrigation ditch one Sunday afternoon when I was eleven years old and received the Holy Ghost that same night. I started playing the piano when I was eleven. A boy named Dennis Burgess played the guitar, and another little girl helped out with an accordion. (She was Marion Vannoy, who later became a missionary to Haiti.) We three children were the music the church had. We worked hard, but the music was usually downright pitiful.

I never gave marrying a minister a thought. When Dennis and I married, he certainly had no plans to be a minister. We were childhood sweethearts who married before we were grown (sixteen and eighteen). We were the first couple married in the new church in Avondale. Mark Baughman was the pastor and performed the ceremony for us.

We were both raised in very strict homes and felt our folks were old fogies. We wanted to do our own thing. We did not have the convictions that our folks had and felt there were a lot of things of the world we could enjoy and still be Christians. We struggled with the will of God, and Dennis spent several years fighting the call of God. He did *not* want to be a preacher! During those years of struggle, we were *very* cold spiritually, and most of the time were actually backslidden at heart. We tried some of the things of the world and looked for excuses to miss church. We made friends with a young sinner couple who influenced us extensively. We found ourselves slipping farther away from God. During this time we had the good fortune to be pastored by Don Dobyns, later missionary to the South Pacific, who was extremely patient with us. I thank the Lord for this man of God who helped us conquer ourselves and eventually surrender to the will of God.

We were married for five years when we finally consecrated ourselves to God and realized that our folks knew what they were talking about. We became very active in the church. Dennis was the youth leader, I led the choir and played the organ, and we both taught Sunday school. Dennis started giving sermonettes that gradually turned into sermons. He would get upset if someone called it preaching. His dad and brother were preachers, and he was sure that God didn't want another preacher in the family. He also had a good job, and God was blessing us financially. We had bought a new home when I was nineteen and he was twenty-one. We knew preachers lived by faith and moved around a lot. We were so happy with our new home and dreamed of living there for years.

In 1969 Mervyn Miller, missionary to England, came by our church and tried to recruit us as Associates in Missions workers to London. He planted the first seed in our hearts for the "regions beyond." We paid a job placement service to help us locate a job in England. There was nothing in England, but we were referred to a company in Lisbon, Portugal. Since there wasn't a church in Portugal at the time, we didn't feel it was the will of God for us to go there.

In 1971 we started making preparation to go to Texas Bible College. When Dennis went in to quit his job, his boss asked him how much he was going to make preaching. When he told him that the salary varied, he asked him how he was planning on taking care of his family with that. He then offered to double his salary if he would stay. We went to Texas Bible College. Our time there was very beneficial, and we learned first-hand what it meant to live by faith.

We were going to evangelize during the first summer break. Don Ikerd, the home missions director of Arizona and today a missionary to South Africa, asked that we preach a revival in a small mining town where he had started an outreach. The Lord blessed us, and we ended up staying three years in Bagdad, Arizona. God poured out His Spirit, and we saw many miracles in this little, remote town at the end of a long, long, isolated road.

We were so thrilled to be able to attend the general conference in Salt Lake City in 1973. That is a real treat for home missionaries! During the foreign missions service, an appeal was made for missionaries, and we both went forward to offer ourselves to God's service wherever He could use us. Brother Dobyns and Brother Ikerd, by now both missionaries, were present and prayed for us. I will never forget the burden and sense of responsibility we felt to prepare ourselves for His service.

We later felt the call of God to Carson City, Nevada, to start another home missions church. That was another story altogether. It was the University of Hard Knocks for us. While we were in Carson City, we were involved in a car accident. I suffered neck and back injuries and was three months convalescing. Only a few received the Holy Ghost, and we were forever fighting city hall. The building codes were very strict, and city officials let us know they did not want us or any other church there. We fasted, prayed, knocked doors, had services in the mall, had evangelists come for revivals, tried every program we had ever heard or thought of, and still did not establish a work.

We were told at a seminar that if we failed to raise up a church in that city, it would be our fault, and that if we would pay the price, God would give us a church. We were very discouraged, felt totally defeated, and wondered how we could possibly be in the will of God. We suffered financially while trying to pay the bills of the church and home. I drove a school bus, and Dennis drove to Reno to work as a welder. We had a very fine couple to help us, Rick and Pat Ruthstrom. For various reasons, however, after three years we were still on square one.

We stayed as long as we felt we should, even though we were offered other opportunities. We finally left when we couldn't endure anymore and felt God release us. When we left, we felt totally defeated and certainly did not feel that we were potential foreign missionaries. Looking back from today's perspective, we can see the value of the lessons we learned and appreciate God's purpose in it all. We definitely didn't see it then!

We are thankful that after Carson City, God led us to the church in Chowchilla, California. Pastor Vaughn Morton of Fresno, California, was a real encouragement to us and repeatedly reminded us of Matthew 10:14: "And whosoever shall not receive you, nor hear your words, when ye depart out of the house or city, shake off the dust of your feet." It helped us to heal from the defeat we felt from the treatment received in Nevada and to realize it was not our fault.

We pastored in Chowchilla for almost three years and again felt God's blessings on our lives. In January 1980, we had a missionary service with Joseph Domingues, who served in Brazil and also many years in Portugal. During this service God moved in a special way. The course of our lives and the lives of our children were changed. At the close of this service God touched our fifteen-year-old son, Ken, in a definite way.

We had totally dismissed the thought of being foreign missionaries even though the burden remained. We avoided the foreign missions services at general conference because we did not want to feel the pain of having a burden for foreign missions while never being able to go. In the service with Brother Domingues, however, a sister in church came to me, bawling, while I was playing the organ and told me that I would be going to the mission field. It was totally out of character for her.

At the same time, God spoke to Dennis and said, "Now is the time." He responded by telling God that if it was really Him, he would have to deal with the entire family. After church we went out to eat with the missionary. Brother Domingues asked Ken if God had spoken to him in the service. Ken began to cry and said, "I feel that God has called me to be a foreign missionary someday." Needless to say, we all started crying as we shared how God had dealt with each of us in the service. There were so many tears that the waitress must have thought someone had died.

At that time, I was a successful home interior displayer. We had everything I had dreamed of—a beautiful home, a new car, a good church, and kids serving the Lord and happy in school. Nevertheless, I wanted to do God's will more than anything.

We now felt the Lord had definitely confirmed His will for us to enter foreign missions. We had a burden, we were ready to sell out and say, "Yes, Lord," but we had no idea of where the Lord wanted us to go. Brother Domingues presented the need in Belgium and encouraged us to call the foreign missions director, Harry Scism, and ask for an application. We filled out the preliminary application, asking to go to Belgium.

Since we had Hispanic people coming to our church, Dennis had started studying Spanish several months before. As we sought the Lord, He gave us direction and we knew we would be going to a Spanish-speaking country. When we filled out the formal application, we asked to go to Argentina or any other Spanish-speaking country where there was a need. In May 1980, we met the Western District Board and were approved by them. We flew to St. Louis to meet the Foreign Missions Board the next day, and they approved us to go to Argentina.

God has reconfirmed His will in our lives many times through the years. We were the fourth missionary family appointed to Argentina. By the time we arrived in

Argentina in 1982, after ten months of deputation and ten months of language study in Costa Rica, two of the missionaries had terminated. We received our permanent residence visas to Argentina during the war over the Falkland Islands. Everyone was sure we would not be able to go to Argentina, and we were asked to consider another field. The Lord gave us another confirmation and put His seal of approval on our lives when we received our permanent residence visas in one day.

At the time of our appointment our two sons, Ken, sixteen, and Kevin, eleven, were very excited about going to Argentina. Our first deputation was a real tour of the United States, and we look back on it with fond memories. Nevertheless, my greatest apprehension was for my children; I felt that it would have been easier to go with smaller children. We had dedicated them to the Lord as babies, and the Lord had to remind me that He is able to keep what we commit into His hands. He has been more than faithful. I have felt His assurance time and time again that He can take better care of my children than I can.

Ken returned to the United States when he was nineteen and went to Texas Bible College. The first thing on the agenda when we got home for our first furlough was a wedding: Ken married Kay Smith. Later Kevin returned to the United States when he was eighteen and also went to Texas Bible College. The first thing on the agenda when we got home for our second furlough was a wedding: Kevin married LeEllen Hodgson. Both boys graduated from Texas Bible College and are in the ministry. Ken and Kay spent twenty-eight months in Argentina and Paraguay on the AIM program and today are fully appointed missionaries to Argentina. Kevin and LeEllen assisted Norman Hamby in Rodgers, Arkansas, evangelized, and are now assisting Dan Rigdon in Plano, Texas.

God definitely prepared us for foreign missions service through every phase of our lives. Looking back over the past sixteen years as foreign missionaries, we can all say that our lives have been enriched. It has not always been easy, of course, and there are still many days of homesickness. No one enjoys being so far removed from family, especially as our parents grow old and pass from this life. We were so sad when Dad and Mom Burgess passed away. We have always been close, and they were such an inspiration to me. While on deputational travel, we have heard people say that they could never be a missionary because their family is very close. Our families are also very close, but Dad Burgess said we could live next door to him, not be in the will of God and miss heaven, but if we do God's will, all of us will be together for eternity. We thank God for this hope.

We have been privileged to serve the Lord in three nations of South America, and I can truly sing one of my favorite songs: "If I had it to do all over again, I'd serve Jesus every day of my life." I can also say that I would be a missionary. I would not trade the beautiful experiences I have had on the mission field for anything in the world. I have seen hundreds filled with the Holy Ghost and their lives changed by the mighty power of God. It is so beautiful to see many of the girls I have taught in Bible school on the mission field go on to become successful mothers and pastors' wives. I am so happy as we look back over the years. All of our family can say we have been blessed abundantly. There is nothing in the world like the contentment in knowing that you are in the will of God. If I had it to do all over again, I'd serve Jesus every day of my life, for He is so faithful!

After sixteen years of excellent missionary service, the Lord brought Brother and Sister Burgess home to serve Him in Rawlins, Wyoming.

A virtuous woman is a crown to her husband (Proverbs 12:4).

Hugs for two little girls that are named after me. The one on my left is a real miracle. The doctors had told her mother she would never have children. Patricia is the first of four that the Lord has given this pastor and his wife.

Teatime at a ladies retreat in Argentina. Patricia Burgess was the ladies president, and Nancy Rivers was the ladies secretary.

*Patricia and Dennis Burgess
singing with daughter-in-law,
Missionary Kay Burgess.*

CHAPTER 4

Marion Vannoy

HAITI AND DOMINICAN REPUBLIC

When I was born in South Pittsburgh, Tennessee, near Chattanooga, my mother was already serving the Lord, but my father was not. He received the Holy Ghost when I was about fifteen. My mother was always a very strong Christian but had many obstacles to overcome because my father was not in the church for so many years.

When I was still very young, we moved to Avondale, Arizona, where there was no church at all. A group of people began to meet for prayer, but we couldn't get anyone to pastor us. Finally Lucille Compton agreed to become our leader and received her minister's license. She did a good job but turned it over to a man as soon as she could. Sister Compton is the mother of Patricia Burgess, who became a missionary to South America with her husband, Dennis. At the time Patty and Dennis were about eleven or twelve. His dad pastored the church some time after her mother began the work.

The church was a small home missions work—just a simple adobe building with a tin roof. Although we were only children, Dennis and Patty played the guitar and piano for the services, while I played the accordion for children's church. This little group was desperate for musicians! But if the Lord could bless a little boy's loaves and fishes, he could bless our young efforts. Today, there is still a good church in Avondale, and the three of us children became missionaries on the foreign field.

I received the Holy Ghost there just after my eleventh birthday during the time Mark Baughman was the pastor. We later moved back to Tennessee, and then I went to Pentecostal Bible Institute in Tupelo, Mississippi, where I met my husband, Daniel Vannoy. Before I was married, my mom died of cancer, so my father and I lived alone for two years. Daniel and I were married a year after I graduated. We both have a four-year bachelor's degree in theology.

Daniel was raised in a minister's home. His grandfather on his mother's side was also a minister, so he had been involved in the ministry from a very young age. He had preached and evangelized quite a lot; during Bible college he evangelized one year instead of working on a secular job.

Of course, I knew before I married him that we would work full time in the ministry. I was very excited about it because I had always been very involved in church work, such as teaching Sunday school, witnessing, and playing music. He also told me before we were married that he had had some thoughts about being a missionary. I knew that his parents had also considered being missionaries at one time, so I was expecting it. But I had the idea that when a ministerial couple finished Bible school, they evangelized for a few months or years until they found a church in the city that they would like to settle in, and stayed there and pastored for a while. Then, if they still felt the call, they would eventually leave that church, having gained ministerial experience, and go to the mission field.

It didn't happen that way with us, however. We were married a year before Daniel graduated from Bible college, and six months after he graduated we were in Haiti on a short-term program. While we were in Bible college, the Glen Smiths showed a slide presentation to the student body. I was at work, but Daniel was determined for me to see it, so he took me to another service they were having in the area. This was the first sign of direction that he had felt. From that time on, he corresponded with Brother and Sister Smith, expressing his interest, and they encouraged him. Although he discussed all of this with me, I can't say that I had a direct call personally, but there were times that I felt assured in my heart that his call was confirmed.

I think it was natural that our families didn't want us to go. Since my father and I had lived alone for two years, it was difficult for me to leave a seventy-year-old dad and go to a foreign country. I felt guilty and told God that He needed to work out something. Then, I became afraid that Dad would die. Of course, God had a much better idea and gave him a wonderful lady whom he married the same month we left.

By this time we had been married a year and a half. Although I was very happy to be in the ministry, I was apprehensive about being a foreign missionary. I hadn't expected us to become involved in foreign missions so quickly, and I wasn't sure I was adequately prepared. Before we went to Haiti for this short-term appointment, my husband had never even flown on an airplane, and neither of us had ever been outside the United States. While on this trip, the flight attendant asked if we were honeymooners. After all, we were a very young couple en route to the Caribbean, but we were going to work for the Lord, not to please ourselves.

We left for Haiti in January 1976 and lived there for six months with a national pastor, Auguste Porisienue.

Since there had never been a resident United Pentecostal missionary in Haiti, there were no facilities for missionaries. Brother and Sister Smith came with us for four or five days and then left us with Brother Auguste, and we began getting acquainted with our new country. After six months, we returned to the United States. That same year we met the Foreign Missions Board at general conference and were appointed as full-time missionaries. In April 1977, while we were on deputational travel, our baby girl, Dana, was born, so we call her our "deputation baby."

While I was still expecting Dana and traveling, I received a letter from Sister Smith telling me how concerned she had become about our housing when she learned I was going to have a baby. God gave her a dream that quieted her fears. In her dream she saw a little white house. Its appearance was very distinct in her mind. I didn't see how this dream helped her, but I was happy to know that she was concerned and praying for us.

When we finished our travel, we went to France to study French, the official language of Haiti. This meant more good-byes, only this time our families were more concerned because we were taking Dana. She was the second grandchild on both sides but my father's first and only granddaughter, so it was very difficult to separate her from him. Of course, it is always difficult to leave aging parents—Dad was now seventy-two—for fear you may never see them again.

In France we finally had a home of our own, even though it was very simple. Robert and Belinda Filkins were also in language school that year. They had three little girls, and we had Dana, so they had a live baby doll to play with. The Filkinses went to Ivory Coast after language school. Brother and Sister Allard, missionaries to Africa, had been there the year before but were delayed because of a severe car accident, so they were also in language school with us for several months.

By the time we finished language school, Dana was

over a year old. We were ready to go back to Haiti, even though we knew by experience that it was one of the most backward countries in the world. I had fears about taking my baby there. I was concerned mostly about the lack of adequate medical care. I was not as concerned for her education because there was a very good accredited Christian school. Many of the children from the American embassy went there instead of to the embassy school. In spite of my fears, I had already settled with the Lord that I would go and felt as ready as I would ever be.

Brother and Sister Smith met us at the airport in Haiti and helped us find a car. Afterwards we went house hunting. We drove around and around, since we were not acquainted with anyone who could help us. We had been searching for some time when suddenly Sister Smith called out, "Glen, Glen! That's the house right there. Stop!" He asked, "What on earth are you talking about?" She started shaking me and saying, "My dream, my dream!" Then I remembered her letter. She continued, "That's it. That's the house I saw in my dream while you were on deputation."

We stopped and asked about the house. Sure enough, it was available! I realized that the Lord was with us and had prepared the way before us. It also made me feel very good that although the Smiths did not live in Haiti and were a long way from us, they were still concerned about us.

A second child was born to us on October 2, 1979. He was a red-headed boy born on Brother Vannoy's birthday. We named him Nathan Daniel and were so happy to have him, but our joy quickly turned to deepest sorrow when he only lived one day. He died in the hospital in the nursery of choking on something due to the nurses' neglect. My nurse went in and found him dead and the nursery nurses asleep.

This was an *extremely* difficult time for us, and we just could not understand why this had happened to us. We brought our baby home for burial. It was a time to be with family and a time to begin to heal to a small degree, but when we returned to Haiti and left the airport to drive home, the most horrible grief came over me. I felt as if I absolutely could not bear to go back into that house, because everything came back to me again. I knew my husband was hurting as well.

It was a terrible struggle not to let bitterness come into my heart against the country and the people, because I felt that their negligence in providing facilities and proper training in the medical field had caused the tragedy. I knew I couldn't let this feeling affect my attitude toward the people we were working with, for it would hinder our ministry to them. I knew God gave His Son for me, and I could not allow myself to become bitter because trying to help these people had cost me my son. I had to learn to leave the situation in God's hands and trust Him. The Lord gave us strength. We learned to lean on Him daily for strength and comfort.

Even though it seemed unendurable, we did go home. Brother Vannoy went to the landlord to pay our rent. The man had always been very nice before, but now he became rough and demanded that we pay a great deal more than we had been paying. This demand, on top of everything else, was very upsetting. We had no idea where we could find another house. I called an Australian friend, and she just happened to know of an available house. When we checked it out, it seemed too good to be true. It was a brand-new home and was just what we wanted, and it cost only a little more than what we had originally been paying for the other house. Within days, we moved out of the house that brought back such sad memories and into a lovely little home that God had prepared for us.

We stayed on the mission field until the end of our term, which was at the end of 1980. After much prayer, we decided that we should not return to Haiti but would stay in the United States to get some pastoral experience, which my husband had never had, although he had evangelized quite widely.

We felt that we really needed a rest, which we did not get. We went to New York City and took a church a half block off Broadway. We pastored there four years. It was a tremendous learning experience—as much as I have ever learned on the foreign field. There were many different cultures in our church. It was an English-speaking church, but we had Puerto Ricans, Jamaicans, Grenadans, Poles, Czechs, and so on. Brother Vannoy was also the foreign missions director for New York during that time, which meant that he scheduled services for missionaries. We always had a lot of missionaries in our home, which we loved.

I never thought that we would go back to the mission field. The church was doing well, and we bought a little house in Queens. We had a difficult time financially because we had never owned our own house and complete furniture.

We had been in New York two years when a precious little boy was born to us. We named him Philip. He had his own little bed and things that we had never had with Dana. We had been traveling on deputation and were always staying in someone else's home, so it was a long time before she had her own little room. Our little Philip was healthy and strong, and we were so thankful to the Lord. The church adored our children, for it had been over thirty years since they had had a pastor who had a baby.

My husband began to feel God dealing with him during prayer that we should return to the mission field. In 1983, we filled out an application to meet the Foreign Missions Board, but a week before the general conference we called and canceled. We felt it wasn't the time. Our church was not ready. Nevertheless, during the next year strong feelings for missions came over me at odd times.

We finally got a nice sofa bed and living room furniture in April, and I was enjoying fixing up my home. One morning I put Philip in a stroller to go down the street to some nearby yard sales, and I took Dana with me. The stroller was an old-fashioned type with a large flat top to keep the sun off the baby. At the yard sale, I found an old, very large picture that was very cheap. I wasn't interested in the picture itself, but the frame was very pretty. My husband enjoys painting, and I was hoping to inspire him to start again.

Since I thought he might like the frame, I bought it, laid it on top of the stroller, and walked home. When I tried to go through the door of the house, the picture hit the door and fell off. The frame fell apart, the picture fell out, and some other pictures fell out from behind it. One was a picture of a downtown marketplace in Haiti called Iron Market; the other was of Kenscoff Market, also in Haiti.

When my husband came home, he could hardly believe it, and we wondered if the Lord was trying to talk to us. After much prayer, he asked the Lord, "If You want us to return to Haiti, please have two men involved in foreign missions talk to me about it." In just a short time Harry Scism, the director of foreign missions, and Glen Smith, the field superintendent for the Caribbean, both contacted him. Our answer was, "Yes, we will return."

We met the Foreign Missions Board in October 1984 and were appointed to return to Haiti. (I did at least have my new furniture to enjoy for six whole months.) It was difficult to leave our church and the people we loved, but as a minister's wife I felt my main role was to be a good wife and mother, support my husband, and help him to fulfill his ministry.

Although there will always be pain concerning the events that happened in Haiti, I have no regrets over having followed the Lord and my husband to the foreign field. The experiences helped me to develop better priorities and values, to be flexible and less concerned with self, and to relate to other people in their problems and heartaches.

I have learned to be a much better and willing handmaiden of the Lord and to be submissive to His will. He has become not only my Savior but also my Lord. He has been what I cling to when all else is gone. I have learned that He is enough. My trust and faith have grown since I have learned that while the nurses were asleep, Jesus was awake and gently came and took my son to be with Him. I love Him. He is worth it all!

The Vannoys spent another term in Haiti and the Dominican Republic before the Lord moved them once more. They presently pastor in Antioch, Tennessee.

And Simeon blessed them, and said unto Mary . . . a sword shall pierce through thy own soul also (Luke 2:34-35).

Marion Vannoy and a lovely Haitian bride, also becoming a pastor's wife.

Marion Vannoy and three-year-old Dana with refrigerator purchased by the Women's Division.

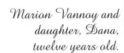

Marion Vannoy and daughter, Dana, twelve years old.

Marion Vannoy and Sister Jules, a devoted Christian and pastor's wife.

CHAPTER 5

Anonymous

I was born into a middle-class family, and my parents were of no particular denomination. We visited churches only on special occasions. My impression was that church was a place with many rules and regulations. Who needed it?

I was fairly content in our home and would have liked to have been a real daddy's girl, but his job kept him away from home too much of the time for that. I had friends and was close to my mother, but I wanted to be close to my father.

I was in the fifth grade when my parents divorced. Although I knew they fought all the time, the divorce came as a total shock to me. It was not that my father left my mother; he had deserted *me!* After the divorce, he rarely came around. Because she was forced to go to work, I felt I had also lost my mother. I was also forced to take on adult responsibilities, for which I wasn't prepared.

As time passed, I saw less and less of my father. The divorce was difficult for my mother, for she had no choice but to take us to a lower-class neighborhood because of her lower income. This put me into contact with many bad influences.

My mother began to date and left me with no adult in the home. Being alone was frightening, and it began to affect me in various ways. One reaction was that I began to steal. I stole things for myself and also would take orders from friends for whatever they asked me to get for them. I did it to get some of the attention I had begun to crave. One time the school chose me to be a safety monitor, and I looked forward to the prestige and attention I would gain. Unfortunately, I stole something and got caught, so I was not allowed to take the position. I was humiliated and didn't want to return to school, where I would be known as a thief and be rejected again.

After my mother remarried, unknown to her I began to drink when I was in the seventh grade. I also experimented with various drugs, though I didn't get as involved with drugs as with alcohol. I began stealing more, lying, cheating on my schoolwork, skipping school, and staying out most of the night at parties, all of which contributed to failing grades in school. I was doing nearly anything to feel accepted by someone—anyone!

Shortly after my mother's remarriage, my stepfather became very abusive, especially to her. At first he was only verbally abusive to me, but then it progressed to slapping and throwing me across the room. Just prior to this I had begun to straighten up somewhat and had almost finished high school.

When my stepfather's drinking became worse, so did his abuse. Sometimes the police had to be called to restore order. Finally one night after a particularly brutal experience, I decided I couldn't take any more and ran away from home without taking anything with me. I wasn't interested in anything except getting away from a man I bitterly hated. Besides my hatred for him, I was also hurt and angry at my mother because she chose him over me.

I went to several different friends, but because they knew my mother they wouldn't help me or become involved, especially since I was still under age. The lack of help from people I had thought I could count on, increased my feelings of rejection.

I was so sure my father had no interest in me whatsoever that it never crossed my mind to call him for help. After trying one "friend" after another, I was finally forced to go to the police and ask for their help. Through their assistance I was placed in someone's home, and my mother helped me some, but I had to work part time to meet my expenses.

These events took place just before my senior year in high school. That summer, I began a downward spiral at a breakneck speed. I drank nightly, danced and partied all night, and tried to do anything to keep from thinking and hurting. As I made the rounds and saw all the unhappy people and their forced laughter, I began to think, There just *has* to be more to life than this!

I decided to get in touch with my dad. I wanted to tell him where I was to emphasize his failure to contact me. I made up my mind that if he started talking to me about God or the church he had begun to attend, I would let him know in a hurry what he could do with his church. I did visit him, and then, most reluctantly, I went to a United Pentecostal Church with him.

During the service, a message in tongues and interpretation came forth. I felt that God was speaking directly to me. For the first time in many years I felt peace, love, and acceptance. I felt that God was drawing this hurting and desperate girl into His arms, where I knew I would find what I had been looking for. No one needed to talk me into giving my life completely over to the Lord. I was more than ready to begin a new, clean life. I was soon baptized in Jesus' name and fervently sought the Holy Ghost for several days.

When I asked God why I was not receiving the Spirit, the Lord showed me that I had deep hatred and bitterness toward my stepfather and that He could not enter into such a heart. I deeply repented and with God's help was finally able to truly forgive my stepfather. I also forgave my mother, but it wasn't until years later, after I had matured, that I truly understood how she had suffered through more than she had been able to handle. She had been desperately trying to survive financially and emotionally, and my actions had not helped her any more than hers had helped me!

As soon as I was free from the anger and hatred, I received the wonderful baptism of the Holy Ghost. I began my new life in God with the same intensity that I lived before I came to the Lord. After finishing high school, I felt a strong desire to go to Bible college. I couldn't get enough of God and was so hungry to learn more and more about the One who had lifted me out of the deadly quicksand of sin.

While at Bible college I met a young man who was already a minister. Because I liked him so much, I felt I needed to reveal my past to him before our relationship went any further. In this way he would be able to decide whether or not someone of my background was suitable girlfriend material. He was very reassuring, and I became convinced that he could really care for me even though I felt I wasn't the caliber of the other young ladies on campus.

Our relationship moved quickly, and a proposal of marriage came *much* sooner than I expected. I loved him and did not hesitate for one moment to say yes. Almost immediately and unbelievably, for the first time in our relationship it hit me that marriage to him, a minister, meant that I was to be a minister's *wife*.

Fear gripped me! How could *I* fulfill the role of a

preacher's wife? I knew nothing of God's Word and barely even knew who God was since I had only given my life
to him about a year earlier. I couldn't fix my own hair,
play the piano, or sing. What qualities did I have to make
me worthy or qualified for this position?

I desperately struggled with my new dilemma, but God
quieted my fears when He spoke these words to my heart:
"I would not have placed you in a position to become a
minister's wife if you were not capable of fulfilling the
role." Being so frightened by my quickly approaching new
position in life, I clung tightly onto the words He had given
to me. After such a short time since giving my life to God,
I found myself an assistant pastor's wife.

Before long my heart began to be gripped and burdened during missionary services. I would weep for the
lost world, but I never realized that one day I, too, would
be a missionary's wife.

We assisted for several years and then accepted the
pastorate of a church. Once again I felt inadequate. Since
we had now been in the ministry several years, I knew
many other pastors' wives. I began to compare myself
with them and wondered how I would be able to measure
up to my new role. I found myself caught up in trying to
win the approval of our congregation.

When it was time for our first visiting missionaries, I
was scared to death. My house wasn't good enough and
my abilities in entertaining were not good enough; *I*
wasn't good enough! I felt like a failure and did not give
myself a chance to succeed. The missionary family was so
kind and easy to be with, however, that the experience
was a wonderful success.

In time I realized that there was far too much pressure
in trying to be what I wasn't. If I was going to be a happy
and successful pastor's wife, I had to be just *me*.

My interest in missionaries and my deep burden for
the lost world grew greatly during our first year of pastoring. One night we were in a missionary service at

another church, and God spoke to my heart, "One day you will go to the mission field." I thought for a moment that I must be crazy. But the message was so strong—as if it were branded onto my heart. To be sure I wasn't just imagining something, I told God that I was not going to reveal my experience to my husband unless he mentioned it first.

When we returned home that night, my husband immediately told me that he felt God talked to his heart about being a missionary. I began weeping and revealed to him my own impression from the Lord. Then I knew that I had truly heard the voice of God. I wondered for some time why God hadn't talked to my heart about being a missionary long before He did. I now realize that He had to prepare me emotionally before I would be ready to handle what I would one day be called to do.

Over the next several years we prayed much about God's direction in our lives and felt our burden for missions grow deeper and deeper. When my husband felt that the time was right, we began the nine-month process of preparing ourselves for appointment: forms, applications, meetings. It was a very trying time of struggling to make ourselves into acceptable material.

The time came to meet the Foreign Missions Board. I felt ready and extremely eager to begin the life that had become my daily heartbeat. We were absolutely dumfounded when we were turned down but told we could reapply the following year.

I was devastated! All of my deep feelings of rejection surfaced, and I could not stop crying for days. The foreign missions service at general conference was especially dramatic, and the main speaker gave an emotional appeal for people to give their all and go to a foreign field to bring the message of hope to a dying world. At his words entreating someone—anyone—to answer the call, I felt confusion and frustration but above all rejection!

The pain was deep, as if I were being gored and scalded. It created a wild whirlpool of emotion and even anger. I wanted to cry out, "I tried! I offered all and you rejected me! Why are you doing this to me? Why am I not good enough?" It was also extremely painful and humiliating for my husband, but it was my pain that caused him the most grief and concern. Sitting through that service, hearing the plea for people to come offer themselves, and knowing that the missions board didn't want us, was the most painful part of the entire experience.

With the help of God, we did survive, and soon after I learned that I would be giving birth in the near future. Our church experienced a real revival, and God blessed us as He never had before. We made up our minds that we would not let the experience defeat us, but it was only with God's help that we were able to meet the board again.

We determined that we would go forever until they appointed us. Fortunately, on our second attempt we were accepted and appointed. Upon our approval I felt a joy and elation that I had never felt before.

Many times on deputational travel and even on the mission field, I have had to battle those old feelings of inadequacy, but God is always there to remind me that He is in control of my life and will give me all the strength and ability I need to be a missionary's wife. I do not write the pages of the book of my life. The Lord writes every word, or I would surely fail. Many years on the mission field have taught me and confirmed that it is not by might, nor by power, nor by my worthiness, but by the precious Spirit of God that we can and will be all that He wants us to be.

For the Lord hath called thee as a woman forsaken and grieved in spirit, and a wife of youth, when thou wast refused, saith thy God (Isaiah 54:6).

CHAPTER 6

Helen Kinney

FINLAND, RUSSIA, ESTONIA, LATVIA, LITHUANIA, AND AUSTRIA

On June 15, 1946, I was born into the family of Samuel and Mary Paisley of Gagetown, New Brunswick, Canada. I was the fourth of five children. My dad was a blacksmith and a heavy drinker. One day he went to the city of Fredericton (about forty-five minutes from home) to do some shopping for his business. While walking down the street under the influence of alcohol, he noticed a young crippled man on the sidewalk selling some religious things. Out of sympathy for the young man, he purchased a little sign that read "Jesus Saves."

As he walked up the street, he became ashamed of the sign and didn't want anyone else to see what he had. He even tried to put it under his other purchases. But every time he tried to put it out of sight, his conscience would smite him, and before he knew it, he would have it on top of his other articles again. He had been raised in a religious home, and he was always taught that he should never lay anything on top of God's Word. Thus he felt guilty every time he tried to put the little sign at the bottom of his purchases.

As he was walking along drunk, a lady saw him and the sign he had. She stopped him and asked, "Young man, do you know what that sign means?" He made some remark to her and kept on his way.

When he arrived home later in the day with his purchases, the older children saw the colorful sign and took it to play with it. My mother told him that the Pentecostal people had been there while he was gone and wanted to know if he would put in his shop an announcement of revival services in their church. He took the announcement and then noticed that the children were playing with the sign he had purchased. He picked it up as well and went to the shop. He placed both the announcement and the sign up on the wall together. As he would turn the forge and work, he saw "Jesus Saves," and then he would see the announcement about the revival services.

It kept going over and over in his mind, so he decided to attend a service and see what it was like. He was much impressed and also convicted, and he surrendered his heart to the Lord. Many were the nights he had come home drunk and my mother would wait up for him, help him get the horses in the barn, and then see him safely to bed. But when he started going to church and came home at night happy and singing, it made my mother angry. She would go into the house, slam the door, and go to bed.

In February, in the cold of the winter, my father was baptized in Jesus' name through a hole cut in the ice. My mother was very upset, since my dad had had some problems with pneumonia previously, and she was sure that he would die after coming out of that icy water. But God looked after him, and he didn't have any problems at all.

My mother could see there was a change in him. My dad sought earnestly for the Holy Ghost. The Lord showed him that he was hindered because he wasn't speaking to a man several miles away. My father got on the bus, went to the man, made things right with him, and then again asked God for the Holy Ghost. The Lord then showed him something else he needed to repent about. Finally one night while he was asleep, my mother awoke and heard him speaking in a strange language. She realized that he was not awake, and she realized he had been filled with the Holy Ghost. She could no longer doubt. She surrendered her life to God, she was baptized in Jesus' name, and she, too, received the Holy Ghost.

I don't recall those days, since I was very young when both my parents got in the church. The only thing I can recall about their life before salvation was the last time we went to the county fair. My father had prize jump horses that he always entered in the fair. That last night we went, my dad told us children that he felt it would be our last time to the fair, as he was convicted about it and would not be attending anymore. I was probably about five years old at that time.

When I was six, my dad began to preach, and from that time on, I was raised in a pastor's home. Many times I have thanked the Lord for His mercy and goodness to our family and that I never knew what life in this sinful world was really all about.

I gave my life to God when I was eleven years old. How well I remember the Sunday night in September 1957 when God dealt with my heart and I made my way to the altar. I was baptized on June 15, 1958, my twelfth birthday, and in July of that year God filled me with the Holy Ghost.

When I was about thirteen or fourteen, the Bill Drost family, missionaries to South America, came to our church. In that service God spoke to my heart about foreign missions. From then on whenever I was asked what I planned to do in life, my answer was, "I'm going to be a missionary." That call guided and kept me all through my teenage years. Even though sometimes I made mistakes, that call would always come back to me and make me think of what I was doing.

Later, as I reached eighteen or so, the call didn't look quite so attractive to me as it had in my younger teenage years. I began to shy back from it. I would go to camp meeting and find every excuse I could not to attend the foreign missions service, because I was struggling with that call.

My husband, Harold, was born just a month earlier than I and about 125 miles north of my home. His parents were not in the church, and even though he and his brother and sisters were sent to a United Pentecostal Church Sunday school, none of them got in the church until 1965. All three of the children are now serving the Lord, but their parents both died without giving their hearts to God.

In September 1959, Harold and I were placed in the same seventh-grade classroom and were classmates for three years. Since he was not a Christian, his jokes and ways were not very interesting or impressive to me. I could not stand him! After ninth grade, my father changed pastorates. We moved several miles away, and I gladly forgot that Harold even existed.

In May 1967, I visited my sister in Ontario and attended the youth convention there. She asked me if I knew Harold and told me he was in Ontario going to Bible college. I could hardly believe my ears, knowing his life in school. But he and his brother had moved to Ontario to find work and had begun attending W. V. Cooling's church in Brantford. Both of them had been baptized in Jesus' name and received the Holy Ghost.

At the youth convention I kept looking to see if I could locate him. Of course, after not seeing him for a few years, I knew there would be several changes in our looks and perhaps I wouldn't recognize him. I never could seem to see him, but during the last service, while the preacher was preaching, I heard someone shouting and recognized his voice immediately. After the service he came to where I was and we had a wee chat. During that chat, something stirred within me and I was attracted to him. I left to go back to New Brunswick to my job and didn't see him again while in Ontario.

Prior to the youth convention, the Lord had dealt with me about quitting my job and moving to Ontario to help in a home missions church. One home missions pastor and his wife had talked to me while I was in Ontario and told me they had a definite need for some music and Sunday school help. So when I went back home, I began to fast and pray and ask God to give me direction as to whether it was His will for me to move to Ontario. After feeling a definite direction to do so, I resigned my job and moved to Ontario in July 1967.

When I arrived there, it was camp meeting time, so I went every night to the services. Harold wasn't there during the week because he was working, but on Friday night he came. We met again, and he asked if he could treat me at the booth.

On Saturday afternoon he asked me to go for a ride with him, which I did. I was from a district that had severed its affiliation with the United Pentecostal Church International for a few years, and during that time several preachers had been preaching in New Brunswick who didn't entirely believe the doctrines as we teach and believe. So I thought I would check Harold out. While driving along that day, I casually asked him, "Do you believe all the doctrine they are preaching at this camp meeting?"

Shocked, he turned to me and said, "What doctrines are you talking about?"

I said, "All this stuff that people have to be baptized in Jesus' name—do you really believe that doctrine?"

He was quick to assure me that he certainly did believe it, and there was no other way in the Word of God. I strung him on for a few minutes to see if he was solid about it, and then I finally told him that I was only joking,

that I, too, believed it with all my heart. But after seeing
so many who were weak on the message, I determined to
know what this guy really believed before I got involved
with him. He had already asked me for a date the following week after the camp meeting was over, and I decided
there was no sense in wasting time on someone who
didn't believe the truth. He was definitely relieved after I
told him I was joking. At first, I thought he was going to
stop, put me out on the side of the road, and let me find
my own way back to the campground!

I had also seen many guys find a girl at camp meeting
just to have someone to sit with in services, but then once
camp was over they would show no further interest. So I
told the Lord, "Lord, if this guy asks me to sit with him
one time during the services, I will know he is not the one
for me." When it came time to go to the tabernacle for
service, he would kindly say to me that he had enjoyed
our time together, but he was going to service and would
meet me at a certain spot afterwards.

During the last Sunday night of camp, I decided to see
if he was interested in me, or if his main interest was the
Lord. I had dated several fellows previously, and I was
ready for a serious relationship, but I didn't want to get
interested in the wrong guy. I watched him as he wor-
shiped and responded to the preaching. I felt he was sincere and dedicated, but I wanted to be sure.

When the altar call was given and we all went to the
front to pray at the close of the message, I went to a spot
where I was sure that he could see me. I, too, sought God
and stayed at the altar for a while. But then, when I knew
he was looking my way, I slipped out the side door, bought
an ice cream cone, came back, and stood just outside the
open door where I knew he could see me. While he was
still praying with someone to receive the Holy Ghost, I
stood, licked my ice cream cone, and chatted with a
friend. Several times he looked my way, but he just kept
right on praying and stayed until the person he was pray-

ing with had finished. It was rather daring of me to test him in this way, but I said, "Thank You, Lord. I know that this guy really is dedicated to You and not just interested in girls."

The next week we went on our first real date, and both of our hearts flipped! He began pastoring his first church in May 1968, and we were married in July of the same year. Recently we celebrated our thirtieth wedding anniversary, and our lives together have been one big, beautiful love story. How thankful I am to the Lord for a husband who is a genuine, sincere Christian!

After we married, God allowed my husband and me to work in home missions for several years. They were some of the most wonderful and fulfilling times in our lives, and I will always be thankful to God for those opportunities. Sometimes we didn't have much money, but we never went hungry. We always had clothes and a good place to live. How good God has been to us!

Then my husband became the foreign missions director for the Atlantic District. I wasn't too happy about that. I was pleased that he was chosen, but it was a spot that I didn't feel comfortable in. As we got engrossed in that work, however, I really enjoyed it and became very comfortable with it. I said to myself, "There, we've found our spot, and this is why God has always given me such a burden for missions." But a few years later, I was to find out that it was only preparation for the real call that He had placed upon my heart.

In the general conference at Anaheim, California, in 1984, God began to deal with my husband about Europe. In the same service, God began to deal with me, and I could only weep and weep. Since my husband was a foreign missions director, he was needed somewhere to help in the service, and I was sitting with our son in a different area of the building. After the service, my husband told me that God had deeply burdened him about Europe during that service and he felt a special tug in his heart about

Finland. He asked me to help him pray for the nation of Finland. I never told him that God had dealt with me also about Europe in the same service.

When we went home, I heard him speak several times about the need for a missionary in Finland and that we needed to pray for God to send someone there. Every time he mentioned it, something would smite me, and I knew deep down inside that he was feeling more than a burden. I began to look in the encyclopedias and everything I could find to read about Finland. The more I read, the less interested I became. One thing that terrified me was that it was next door to Russia. I told the Lord, "Lord, I'm living close enough to Russia right here in Canada." I never mentioned to my husband that I was reading about Finland or even feeling anything about it.

Each year at our church we had a foreign missions convention. In 1985, at our convention were Brother and Sister Harry Scism, Brother Freeman from Africa, and the Alan Demos family from Greece. Brother Scism asked my husband if he had ever thought about going to the mission field. My husband told him he had a burden for a country, but he had never felt a call.

One day during our convention, he asked Brother Demos if he knew whether anything was being done in Finland. Brother Demos responded, "Why? Is God calling you to Finland?" My husband immediately dropped the topic.

The following week after our missions convention, my husband told me that he felt God was dealing with him about something, but he wasn't sure of just what it was. He was going on a fast until he knew what God was trying to show him. I, too, felt an unsettledness within myself and knew something was happening, so I told him I would like to fast with him.

On the third day of our fast my husband arose early in the morning and told me he was going to the church to pray and that he was going to stay there until the Lord spoke to him. He asked me not to interrupt him for any phone calls unless it was an absolute emergency.

After I got our son off to school, I, too, went to pray. As I walked back and forth across the bedroom praying, I began to say, "Lord, I really don't want to leave this church we are pastoring, but if You are trying to show us that You want us somewhere else, please help me to be mature enough to accept Your will." There were some needs within our district, and I told the Lord, "Lord, even if it is such and such a place, I'll be willing to go." As I said that, I could feel something break within me. Then I told the Lord I'd do another thing if it was His will, and something else broke within me. Then I said, "Lord, even if it is a foreign field, I will be willing to go." Again something greater broke within, and then finally after much internal struggle I said, "Lord, even though it might be Finland, I will go." When I said those words, intercessory prayer came upon me, and I fell on my face on the floor and groaned in the Spirit.

After the intercessory burden finally subsided and I was able to pray normally again, I told the Lord, "I am not the preacher of our family; my husband is. If You want us in Finland, You will have to tell him, because I am not telling him anything about what happened to me this morning in this prayer time."

About 10:30 or so that morning my husband came back from the church. When he came into the kitchen, the first thing he said to me was, "What were you praying about this morning?"

I looked at him rather shocked and answered, "Why, I was praying about several things," and I named a few.

He looked at me again and asked, "But what else were you praying about this morning?"

Again I named some other matters.

He took me in his arms and said, "Honey, what were you *really* praying about this morning?" I knew I couldn't lie to him, but I had told the Lord I wasn't going to tell him what I had been praying about, so I said, "What were you praying about?"

He responded, "I can't tell you, but if God really spoke to me this morning, and I believe He did, then you *were* praying about something very specific this morning."

I said, "You tell me first what you were praying about, and then perhaps I'll tell you."

His reply was, "No, I made a little covenant with God this morning, and it is very important that I know what you were praying about."

Well, after living with this man for many years, I pretty well knew what he was thinking. I realized that God had been dealing with him as well. I began to weep, and I told him what happened to me in prayer.

He then related to me what had transpired at the church. He was on his face on the floor of the platform, weeping and praying, knowing God was dealing with him about Finland. He gave the Lord several reasons why he didn't feel that he could go to this nation, including that he couldn't learn a foreign language. At the back of our church we had a slogan over our Partners in Mission display that read, "The power within us is greater than the task before us." When he lifted his face from the carpet after giving God all the reasons why he couldn't, there was the slogan facing him. God asked him, "Who are you? And who do you think I am?" Finally, he surrendered to God and prayed, "Lord, if you have really called me to Finland and this is truly Your voice I've heard this morning, when I go home to the parsonage I want my wife to have felt this same call and have been praying about the same thing, because, God, we are a team and I can't go without her."

A few days later after things had settled down in our minds, we began to think we had made a terrible mistake, that this couldn't possibly be true. We went to the post office, and there was an envelope from Brother Demos. Inside the envelope was only a photocopy of a Partners in

Missions letter from Brother Tilley in Norway highlighting the need for a missionary in Finland. Brother Demos had seen it on someone's church bulletin board, photocopied it, and put it in the mail to us. Just when our reasoning was doubting it all, God had another little sign to show us He was indeed talking to us.

We decided we would apply to the Foreign Missions Division. When we sat down to fill out the preliminary application, however, it just seemed impossible to do. Finally my husband said to me (I was typing it for him), "Wait, this may be of God, but there is something wrong. This can't be God's time, so let's just set it aside and wait." That is what we did. The application sat until October, and then at the general conference in Texas that fall, we finally felt a release in the Spirit to proceed. At the time, we didn't totally understand it all. But God knew best, and later we saw many reasons why the Lord held us back. We were finally appointed in May 1986, and in the fall we began our deputational travel.

What a privilege it is to have salvation and to serve the Lord! The things that look like such mountains to the flesh are really not so bad, especially when we are walking in the will of God.

And therefore will the LORD wait, that he may be gracious unto you, and therefore will he be exalted, that he may have mercy upon you: for the LORD is a God of judgment: blessed are all they that wait for him (Isaiah 30:18).

Sister Angie Clark, Foreign
Missions Division;
Sister Kinney; Sister Rene,
AIMer to Czech Republic
in Vienna, Austria.

At work in the office.

A group from the Vienna,
Austria, church at the
German/Austrian
Conference, Feburary 1997
in Germany.

Sister Kinney with a
group of Filipino believers,
who presented her with
flowers on her birthday.

CHAPTER 7

Evangeline Rodenbush

GHANA, EUROPE, AND THE MIDDLE EAST

It was a humble beginning. My dad was pastoring a small home missions church near Decatur, Illinois, when I was born. Three years later, our family moved to Cobden, Illinois, and the basement of the small church became our temporary home. A Sunday school room became our bedroom, where Dad built beds for my brother and me, and horror of horrors, the only toilet was outside and down the path.

Every time there was a hard rain, our basement home would flood, and Dad would put our beds and other belongings up on concrete blocks until the water subsided. Those were difficult times for my parents, although I didn't realize it then. I am sure they struggled even to put food on the table. Ice cream, soft drinks, chips, and candy were only for birthdays or special occasions. I had lots of love, though, and Mom and Dad always made us kids feel that it was a privilege to be involved in the ministry no matter what the personal inconveniences might be. I know now that God used all these circumstances as part of my training for the future.

My dad could do anything—literally. He was a butcher, builder, mechanic, preacher, and prayer warrior. With these skills he made a living, kept the old car running, built a great church congregation, and built a parsonage with his own hands in his spare time. To supplement the income, Dad got a job cutting meat at a grocery store on Friday and Saturday. Whenever there was a need he couldn't provide, he and Mom simply went to their knees in prayer.

After several months, I had an unfinished attic room of my own in the new parsonage Dad built, and never again did I have to worry about the rain flooding my room or helping Dad put our things up out of the water. We also now had an indoor bathroom, which was wonderful, especially in the winter.

In time, Dad won to the Lord the owner of the grocery store where he worked. After this man and his wife became a part of our church and realized just how poor we really were, Saturdays became a very special day. We would go to Hinkle's Grocery, and Brother Hinkle would give us a chicken for Sunday dinner and a Coke for each of us to enjoy. Occasionally, he would also allow us to choose a candy bar or some other treat. I never cared much for eating sweets, but I did love salty things, so I would always choose a bag of potato chips. That was a real treat to me!

Cobden is located in the heart of apple and peach country, and migrant workers often came to acquire work. Often these people would come to our door begging. Some were bums by choice, but others were good people who were temporarily in desperate need—even more than we were. One Saturday night, Mom fixed hamburgers, and Dad had brought home from Hinkle's

Grocery a special treat—a large bag of potato chips. I eyed those chips and mentally divided the bag into portions for the whole family. Just as we sat down to this delicious meal, there was a knock at the door, and I'll never forget my despair as I saw that bag of potato chips go to someone whom Dad felt needed some food. I felt mistreated and thought silently, I guess Dad loves them more than me. I didn't mind the sandwiches that he gave them, but, oh, my potato chips! That was one time I wished my dad was not such a generous, compassionate person.

The years passed, God blessed, and the church grew. By the time I was twelve years old, I had become the church pianist/organist and a Sunday school teacher. I also had other interests besides potato chips now—boys! And the guys at youth camp were plentiful. I loved youth camp.

One summer just after I turned sixteen, I was in my dad's cabin on the old campground in Illinois. Mom and I were talking about boys—what to look for and what to avoid. It was lecture time as the guy I had been sitting with in church evidently wasn't her choice. "Honey, right there is a nice young man," she said pointing out the window. I jumped up to take a look and saw Bob Rodenbush walking by.

Tragically, just a few months later, my mom was killed in an airplane crash. Being the oldest at home, I became a mother overnight to my younger brother and sisters. My baby sister was only three years old. Not quite a year later Dad became pastor of the church in Carbondale, Illinois, where Southern Illinois University is located. A young man named Bob Rodenbush was a university student there. I was still sixteen when we began dating.

Bob had acknowledged his call to preach, and he submitted himself to my dad's mentoring. One thing Dad could not endure was anyone whom he considered lazy—and lazy preachers were the worst in his book. He felt that if the Lord called a person to the ministry, he should not sit and wait for the big opportunity. He should start *doing* something!

One night Dad and Bob were traveling together to a special service. As Dad, who was also presbyter, drove through a town called Cutler, he suddenly turned and pulled up in front of an old building that had once been a church but had been closed down for some years due to lack of interest and a pastor. "You say you have a call to preach?" Dad said to Bob. "Here's a good place to start, son. Why don't you see what you can do with this?"

The challenge was accepted by the equally motivated Bob Rodenbush, and within weeks approvals and arrangements were made to open the church. Not having a car, Bob hitchhiked the forty miles to Cutler week after week. He paid past utility bills, cut the window-high grass, cleaned up and remodeled the old building, and began services twice a week. He was nineteen years old.

Bob and I dated off and on during this time for three years. We married with my dad's blessing when I was nineteen and he was twenty-one. I always knew that Dad really liked Bob, and somehow I feel that he might have had a lot to do with our getting married—at least in prayer. I had always hoped to marry a preacher, and Bob certainly needed a piano player in his little church. I felt so good that really he had also been Mom's choice; I wish she could have known that I married him.

Unfortunately, because of past circumstances, the town of Cutler was very suspect toward the young Pentecostal preacher who had come to town. He was not discouraged, however, and after we married we both worked diligently to make our little church attractive and productive. Then one cold winter night in February 1963, our beautiful church caught fire and burned to the ground! We stood in the freezing cold and watched our work and dreams go up in smoke—not even a song book was saved. Many townspeople who came to watch it burn declared that this would be the end of the Pentecostal church.

But they didn't know Bob very well. By 10:00 A.M. that Sunday he had secured permission to hold Sunday school in the fire station. Inspired by his determination and touched by a young preacher's efforts to carry on, the community began to help. Some offered chairs, a pulpit, a piano . . . and at church time that day we were having church. God seemingly used this disaster to rally the people of the town to our aid and turn their hearts toward us. In time a new church and attached parsonage were dedicated. Our church grew to an average attendance of 170 in just a few years. We were blessed financially, and I could buy potato chips any time I wanted. I was happy!

In the winter of 1966 the late J. H. Yohe, Sr. invited Bob to go to Nigeria, West Africa, to talk to a group of Africans who were interested in Jesus Name baptism. On that trip, along with Missionary Jack Langham from Liberia, Bob helped baptize 1,066 Africans in the name of Jesus. They also stopped in Ghana, West Africa, to talk with others who were interested.

While on this journey, Bob sent back cassette tapes to me of some of the services. Something happened to me as I listened to those tapes. A burden swept over me, and I began crying. I couldn't stop. Suddenly I felt as though I belonged to those people and they belonged to me. I felt responsible for their souls. I know now it was the beginning of a call to Africa.

When Bob returned, he too was different. God had placed a heavy burden on both of us for those people. We prayed diligently for God to call someone to go there. There were missionaries in only one country in West Africa at that time, Liberia. No other country had been opened to our church in that part of Africa. We were sure that the Lord would call Brother Yohe to go.

Although I had wanted to marry a minister, it never crossed my mind that the minister I married would be called to a mission field. I always thought that missionaries were different and certainly cut from better material than I. Like most, I didn't think missionaries were exactly human. At that time I didn't understand that missionaries are just ordinary people who are called and willing to work for God in another country. Bob had never mentioned missionary work to me, but later I learned that in his high school year book the seniors wrote what their future would be in twenty years; he wrote, "Missionary."

For two years we continued to pray for Brother Yohe, or someone, to go to West Africa. Then one day while in prayer the Lord asked Bob, "How about you?" When Bob told me, I wasn't surprised because I had strangely and consistently been drawn to the people on the tapes. Not only that, my mother had always taught me, "Your husband's ministry is of primary importance. Wherever God sends him, go willingly, for to be in God's will is the best place you can be." I was willing—but I had a problem.

Bob and I had been married almost six years and wanted a baby, but we had also been told by the doctor that we might never have a child. Just at this time the Lord gave us a beautiful baby boy. This baby was very special to us. As I considered going to Africa, I thought, I can make this choice for myself, but how can I make this decision for our baby? Like any mother, I wanted the best for my boy: cute clothes, the best doctors, the best education, and a thriving church for him to be reared in.

During the time we were waiting, waiting, waiting for the missionary application process to be completed, I was debating, debating, debating within myself about taking our baby boy to Africa. One night when Rob was only a few months old, I was awakened in the night by my baby's cries. I ran to the nursery and pushed open the door. Smoke and a terrible odor enveloped me! I quickly grabbed Rob from his little bed to get him out. I must have screamed, because Bob was right behind me. He saw the pillow that had accidentally been left up against the night light and had begun to smolder. I marveled that my baby had not been asphyxiated by the smoke and stench of smoldering foam, which had begun to fill the house.

Bob threw the pillow into the front lawn. We were safe. But it was 3:00 A.M. and we couldn't stay in the house so we opened all of the windows, got in the car, and began just driving around the countryside. As we drove, waiting for the house to clear, I held my baby boy in my arms and thanked God for sparing his life. My heart was overwhelmed with gratefulness to the Lord for His protection.

Suddenly the Lord spoke to me—not in an audible voice, but very clearly He spoke to my heart, "I am God. I am the giver of life. Whether you are in the United States, where all things seem good and secure, or anywhere in this world, I am still God! I am able to keep what you commit to me." I knew God had spoken directly to my need. That night I committed my most precious possession to the Lord, my baby boy. I have no regrets. God *is* able to keep what we commit to Him.

I was incredibly nervous when we were interviewed by the Foreign Missions Board at the general conference in Atlantic City, New Jersey. We were so young, and they were so dignified! I was afraid they wouldn't appoint us. I was also afraid they would! The night before our meeting, we hardly slept a wink as we went from, "Well, maybe they will turn us down and we can be free to stay home" to "If they turn us down, we'll be heartbroken!" Back and forth our thoughts and prayers went all night. Finally morning came and we found ourselves in the board room. They asked my husband all of the questions except for one to me: "How do you know you are called to Africa?" I answered the best I could.

The foreign missions director at that time was the late Oscar Vouga. He was a good and tender-hearted man inside, but outwardly, to me, he was very intimidating. He came over to where I was sitting and pointed his finger in my face saying, "Young lady, you had better be *sure* you are called, because there *will be* times when that is *all* you will have to go on!" I felt embarrassed and hurt, but now I know that he was right. Many times I've had to recall his words and say, "Thank you, Brother Vouga, you were so right!" We were appointed as the first resident, pioneer missionaries to Ghana, West Africa, in 1968.

There were several times I would have been ready to come home had I not been sure that my husband was called and that we were in God's perfect will. I had also fallen in love with Africa and the people there. During our almost ten years in West Africa there were many trials, inconveniences, and difficulties.

One time my husband's life was threatened, and we felt the situation was very serious. We discussed what to do. Should we leave? Bob began to weep as we drove down the street. "I can't leave here until God tells me to leave," he said. "Even if they pick me up piece by piece off the streets of this country, I'm staying until God releases me! God called me here, and God can keep me." I looked at him and thought, I have never loved and respected you more than I do at this moment.

We stayed and God was with us. Revival swept West Africa. We were privileged to work with those wonderful people to open five countries: Ghana, Nigeria, Togo, Benin, and Ivory Coast. Thousands were baptized and filled with the Holy Ghost. A Bible college was established, and ministers were trained to take the gospel message all across West Africa.

What about the baby boy who was now a missionary kid in Africa? I have no regrets! Rob hardly had a sick day in Africa. He thrived physically and in every way. There was a good school in Accra with an American system and students from many countries. In his third grade class, he had friends from eighteen nations. What a tremendous experience and opportunity!

Rob was eleven when we returned to the United States to accept appointment as coordinator of overseas ministries in the Foreign Missions Division. This was a good age for him to adjust to life back in America with a minimum of problems. At first he attended a church school; later he transferred to a public high school in order to take college credit courses and advanced classes. Our concern for his adjustment was allayed when he graduated from high school as valedictorian in a class of over five hundred students. He was asked to give the opening prayer at the graduation, and when he was introduced by the principal, his classmates began to applaud, whistle, and cheer for him. Tears filled my eyes. I realized that Rob had won the respect of his classmates by quietly and determinedly living a Christian life, and I also realized that God had kept what I had committed to Him.

Rob received an academic scholarship to the University of Missouri and also to Washington University School of Law. Today he is a practicing Christian attorney and wants to use his abilities to help the church and ministry. His testimony is that it is a privilege to be an MK (missionary kid), and he has served as the first president of the MK Association for the Foreign Missions Division. He says he would not be afraid to raise children on the mission field, for "being in God's will is the best place for any kid to be."

Our twelve years of working as coordinator of Overseas Ministers were great years, and our ministry expanded into many areas of foreign missions. During that time Bob initiated and launched the Associates in Missions program with over 600 AIMers serving overseas. He also coordinated all the literature, evangelism, and Bible school training programs around the world and helped in the writing and revision of more than forty textbooks for our overseas schools. He has also served on the Foreign Missions Board since 1978.

One of the most exciting involvements of those days was vernacular radio broadcasts, including China Outreach. We smuggled Bibles into China several times and also helped organize world conferences that one time included taking the group on a trip to China. It was also during these years that we got to be involved in coordinating the annual School of Missions for our missionaries and Compassion Services International for humanitarian relief.

In 1990, Bob was asked to serve as regional director of the Europe/Middle East Region. It was an awesome challenge. Our responsibilities included seventy-two nations with more than 1.2 billion people. From Iceland to the border of Alaska, west to east, and from the North Pole to Saudi Arabia, north to south, the region spans fourteen time zones. It includes Western Europe, North Africa, Russia, all of the former communist countries of Eastern Europe, and the Middle Eastern countries such as Jordan, Egypt, and Israel. In only seven years, twenty-two new countries were opened to the gospel with the help of our dedicated missionary families.

One time when Bob and I were dating, he casually teased, "Stick with me and we'll go places!" That was a prophecy. To coordinate the work in such a large area means keeping on the move. In one year alone, we were in twenty-two countries, made sixty-one airplane flights, made five train trips, and traveled thousands of miles by car. We were gone from our home 244 nights. Through the years we have packed many suitcases, waited for hours in lines and airports, slept in many different beds, chairs, and airplane seats, and suffered continual jet lag. We've had numerous injections, we've eaten all kinds of food, and we've had our experiences with malaria, motion sickness, and, yes, diarrhea. We have ministered in over 125 nations of the world, worked with wonderful missionaries and nationals in many countries, and can truly say, "We are blessed!" Working for the Lord in foreign missions service is the greatest privilege and the most fulfilling and spiritually rewarding experience I could ever hope for.

And I have never lacked for potato chips!

She openeth her mouth with wisdom; and in her tongue is the law of kindness (Proverbs 31:26).

Brother and Sister Rodenbush and Rob in their early years in Ghana, West Africa.

The Rodenbushes arriving in Ghana for second term of missionary service.

▼

Evangeline Rodenbush in African village home.

Brother and Sister Rodenbush and Rob receive gifts of Kente cloth and Ashanti stools in Ghana.

Rob graduates from high school as valedictorian.

Evangeline Rodenbush with Thetus Tenney and other workers passing out Bibles in Bulgaria.

The Rodenbushes are appointed as regional director of Europe/Middle East to replace the retiring regional director, Brother and Sister Robert McFarland.

Evangeline Rodenbush with other regional directors' wives in 1996.

CHAPTER 8

Else Lund

LIBERIA AND GHANA

by Evangeline Rodenbush

Have you ever known anyone so nearly perfect that he or she seemed too good to be true? I have. Her name is Else Lund.

One of the rewards of my going to Africa as a missionary was getting to know and work with Else. Else began her missionary work in Liberia, West Africa, teaching in the mission school way back in the bush in a village called Fassama. In those days there was not even a road to Fassama, because it sits in the middle of the jungle. We had to fly in a small plane to get there.

My first trip to Fassama was in 1969. To fly over that dense jungle is a breath-taking experience, especially when you encounter a tropical rainstorm on the way. In fear I pondered, What is down there, and what if this plane does not make it? But we made it safely, and what an experience to visit the Fassama mission station! Two lady missionaries, Pauline Gruse and Laverne Collins, walked for days through the jungle trails to this African village to open this mission. Sister Collins died there on the mission with malaria. Sister Gruse, being alone, had to prepare her body, build her casket, and bury her. Her grave still holds a prominent place on the mission compound today.

It was to this remote African jungle and village that a beautiful, blonde young lady named Else Lund went to assist Sister Gruse and teach in the mission school. It was in Fassama that I really became acquainted with Else, and immediately I sensed that this was no ordinary person—she was someone very special. I have always said, "If there was ever an angel who lived on earth, it is Else." I don't know of anyone more wonderful, more dedicated, or more of a Christian lady than she.

At this time we were in Ghana, West Africa, pioneering the work as the first resident missionaries to that country several thousand miles away. But as Liberia and Ghana were the only countries in West Africa at that time with missionaries, we felt like neighbors. We kept in touch.

Believing that training nationals to take the gospel to their own people is the real secret to missionary work, Brother Rodenbush did an unusual, unheard of thing in those days: he started a Bible school within three months of our arrival in a brand-new country. In the first Ghana College of Bible class we had ten students, and a small shed with a tin roof and walls was donated to house this humble beginning. Excitement and interest grew, and soon this project became too much for one man to handle. We needed more teachers.

Hearing of what we were doing, Else told us, "I wish I could come and help you. I am teaching reading, writing, and arithmetic, but what I really want to teach is God's Word." We were thrilled to have her join us in Accra, Ghana, in February 1971, where she has since given many, many years of her life teaching what she knows and loves best, God's Word.

Else was born in Dyment, Ontario, Canada, but her father was born in Denmark, and her mother was from Norway. Her ancestors were Danish Lutherans, and some were preachers. There was no United Pentecostal Church in Dyment, but her parents taught her solid principles, the Ten Commandments, and the Lord's Prayer. That was the extent of her religious training.

She went through high school and college in Canada and, after receiving her degree, began teaching at a school near her home. She continued to further her education in Toronto. In August 1963, Else began to get sick. She was experiencing lots of pain in her body but continued teaching her classes. By September, the pain had become so severe that she had to be hospitalized. The fearful diagnosis: polio! Two weeks later her sister and brother were taken from their home in an ambulance with the same illness, polio. Else spent time in an iron lung, but she recovered with only slight physical effects. Her brother suffered greater physical handicaps and is confined to a wheelchair.

In time Else was able to return to teaching school. One day in school, an old friend came by and shared the plan of salvation with her. Soon, she and her sister, Ingeborg, began attending services that were held in an old, abandoned school. The building wasn't much, the music was only a guitar, and the crowd was only about seven, but God's presence was in the place. The pastor in Kenora, Ontario, William Cooling, traveled 180 miles every Friday night to hold services for this small group. Soon Else was baptized in Jesus' name, and two months later, her father, mother, brother, and sister were also baptized. Not long after, Else received the Holy Ghost. She later attended Bible college in Belleville, Ontario, and in St. Paul, Minnesota.

At the early age of ten, Else had a dream in which she

saw many black faces. It was a strange dream to her as she had never even seen a black person in her life. While attending Bible college, she had that same dream again. She began to realize that it was part of her direction and call to missionary work. Several young men were interested in Else, she dated some, and she was even engaged at one time. As God began to work in her life, however, she put all boyfriends and other interests aside. Her only objective became to go to Africa.

In 1962, after graduating from Apostolic Bible Institute, Else returned to her hometown, where she began a Sunday school for all ages in the elementary school. Later she reached out to an Indian reservation about fifteen miles away, and she won the chief and many others to the Lord.

During this time she also made application to the Foreign Missions Division for missionary service, and in January 1963 her dream came true. She left for Liberia, West Africa, to teach school on the mission compound in Fassama, and she taught there for seven years. Certainly she must have suffered loneliness, fear, and disappointment. She also had constant attacks of malaria with high fever that left her weak, tired, and with weight loss. Several times she came close to death. These things had to be learned from others, because Else does not complain. Her family says that in her letters home she told only of the good things that happened and of how many were baptized and filled with the Holy Ghost.

Naturally we were thrilled to have someone like this join our missions team in Ghana. Her passion was to teach the Bible to national leaders so that they could in turn take the gospel to their own people. She taught also in churches, retreats, and seminars. The people came to love her and respectfully called her "Our Teacher." Else Lund knows the Bible better than almost anyone who ever lived, though she would deny it should you give her that compliment. Not only did she sit under the teaching of such great men as S. G. Norris, William V. Cooling, and others, but she loved to study continually. Any time I went to Else's house, most likely I would find her on the couch with study books scattered around her on the floor. It was her favorite thing to do.

One night Ghana was experiencing political unrest, and we were fearful that a military coup might take place. It had happened before during our time there, and we were aware of what to do should it happen: stay in the house and wait for direction from the embassy. We were sitting on Sister Lund's veranda that hot, tropical night talking about the possibilities of a coup when suddenly we heard a massive explosion, and off in the distance we saw smoke and flames billowing upward into the sky. We also heard screaming, and we said to each other, "This is it. The coup has begun." Our house was more protected so we decided that Else should quickly gather together her most valuable belongings, and we should all go to our house to wait it out. We felt we only had minutes, as the explosions were not far from where we were.

"Don't worry about taking anything but my passport and my Bible and that trunk of notes," she said, pointing at a large footlocker. " If you can just save my Bible notes, that's all I care about." Brother Rodenbush carried her precious notes, Rob and I helped carry a few other things, and we quickly headed for our house. The next morning we found out that a gas truck had exploded, and it really wasn't the beginning of the coup (which came later), but I have never forgotten what was really important to Else.

Else was not only a teacher and preacher, she was a dear friend. When I got discouraged or upset about anything, big or small, I knew where to go. Else always had a chocolate cake or something sweet baked. A piece of cake and a cup of coffee with my wise and understanding friend always seemed to lift the load. Maybe the problem would not even be mentioned, but she had an aura of peace about her that calmed my spirit. I always left feeling that I had been in the presence of God. In our nine years of her working closely together with my husband and me, there was never a cross or unkind word. With Else Lund, perfect harmony is possible.

One day Else and I decided to go for a ride. Because the view was so beautiful, one of our favorite places was the University of Ghana. On the grounds was an old clock tower, and from the top was a breathtaking view. In this tower was an ancient elevator that was condemned, unreliable, and risky. We couldn't use it until we signed our name stating that the university was not responsible if anything should happen. Else is adventurous and fearless and she said, "Let's go." I agreed, not because I am fearless, but because I thought to myself, I will be safe as long as I am with Else, because God would never allow anything to happen to someone so needed and wonderful as she. I knew God didn't owe me anything, but somehow I felt I would be safe as long as I was with Else. We made it up and back down again, safely! In other experiences when we all faced danger and crisis, I always felt comfort and confidence when Else was there.

It was a sad day when the Rodenbush family left Ghana and Else to take up other responsibilities with the Foreign Missions Division. Our son, Rob, still calls her Aunt Else. She will always hold a special place in our hearts and our lives. Else has not only worked with us in West Africa but shared her unique teaching abilities with more than thirty different missionary families in other African countries such as Liberia, Nigeria, Togo, Benin, Ivory Coast, and Cameroon.

In 1996 she was honored in a special celebration for her twenty-five years as a missionary to Ghana. Missionaries Jim and Linda Poitras led this silver jubilee celebration. Over six thousand Ghanaians were in attendance, and guests came from far and near. They poured out their hearts in love with verbal expressions and laid more than forty gifts at her feet. She was also officially titled "Queen Mother of the United Pentecostal Church of Ghana" in a Ghanaian ceremony where she was presented with an Ashanti stool and Kente cloth.

If ever anyone was deserving of this love and honor, it was Else. Jim and Linda Poitras told me, "Revival and church planting are dear to her heart, along with her teaching. What church in Ghana has been built and had a need and has not been blessed with her generosity? The ladies of Ghana know her kindness and concern even to the point of her bringing them drinking water when water was scarce. The youth also have felt her love and have been guided by her faithful teachings. Many of them are now ministers and workers in the kingdom. Every ordained minister in the United Pentecostal Church of Ghana has sat under her teaching in Bible school, and the total work has greatly benefited, becoming strongly established in truth. Everywhere Else has traveled, she has left the people with a deeper understanding of biblical truths and a greater revelation of the things of God. Dobro, Lortuedor, Patu-Kope, and Prampram are some of the churches that have been established as a direct result of her ministry."

Total commitment and dedication to God and His will is her motto in life. She heard the voice of God possibly at only ten years of age, and she has never turned back. The Poitrases wrote, "War couldn't stop her (she was on the last commercial flight out of Liberia when the civil war was going on); hot tropical heat, dirt roads, rain, and dust never kept her home; recurring malaria and other serious health problems have never slowed her down for long; hardship and inconveniences never deterred her; political unrest and coups couldn't diminish her commitment; even church crises could not kill her love and compassion for the people. At times she has worked completely alone in Ghana under very dangerous and adverse circumstances. She is truly more than a conqueror through the grace of Jesus Christ. I doubt if there is anyone in all of West Africa more loved than she. Only eternity will reveal the true value and influence of her life and ministry. Exalting herself would be unthinkable to her."

I feel honored to call Else Lund my friend. She is a truly dedicated missionary and a faithful Christian lady— and she is a lady in every sense of the word. She has a humble and quiet spirit. Even though she has accomplished more than most in her lifetime and thousands will rejoice in heaven because of her life and ministry, for her to exalt herself or get out of her place would be unthinkable to Else. No wonder she is so loved. She also has a forgiving spirit, so I'm sure she will forgive me when she learns I have written this chapter about her.

Let each esteem other better than themselves (Philippians 2:3).

Else Lund receives Ashanti stool and other gifts from Ghanaians.

Else Lund and Nona Freeman in Ghana.

CHAPTER 9

Corliss Nilsen

NORWAY AND SWEDEN

The missionary was a very exciting and a very special person to me from the time I was a small girl. I had decided that when I grew up I would become a missionary. Of course, that was only a childish dream, as I was in no way a Christian. As a teenager, my ideas completely changed, and I had no desire to be a missionary nor even the slightest intention of being a Christian. It wasn't until after my twentieth birthday that my whole life turned around and I met my Lord and Master, Jesus. That was when my new life began.

As a new Christian, everything was exciting, and I was open to everything in the work of the Lord. All the dreams of my childhood came back, and I dreamed of doing a work for Him. When I was asked to be a substitute teacher for a Sunday school class, I was so excited.

A few months later I met my husband-to-be. He was in

the navy and a very fine Christian. He was also just as excited about the work of the Lord. As we talked, he shared his dreams of doing something for God. Once, very casually, he mentioned going to a mission field, but it was soon forgotten.

As the years passed, we felt led to go to North Dakota and take over a one-year-old home missions work. I was thrilled, for this was where I had been raised. Much of my family lived about eighty miles from the church we were going to pastor. After about four years of pastoring in North Dakota, I started to see my mother and many of my relatives come to the Lord. As far as I was concerned, my life was complete. I couldn't be happier. I had three children, a wonderful husband, my relatives in the church, and a nice home. I had everything a woman could ask for.

Then, my husband told me that he felt a call to go to Norway. Weeell, I thought to myself, he has had these different feelings before, and *they* didn't work out. Surely this will be the same. I passed it off, but he just wouldn't forget about it. I tried every way I could to forget it. I could tell he wasn't himself and thought he must be sick, so I begged him to have a complete physical. He finally agreed, but there wasn't a thing wrong with him (until he got a look at the doctor's bill, that is). He continued talking about Norway

Finally I decided I'd better have a talk with Jesus. I told God that if this call was real, then He needed to give me some sort of burden also, because I hated every thought of it. To leave my mother, when she was a new convert, was unthinkable! We were really good friends again after eleven years in opposite corners. I *couldn't* leave. No, no, no!

One day a lady from our church visited, and we listened to a record. The song "Take My Name" came on. As we listened, I heard not just "Take My Name" but "Take My Name to Norway"! The feeling was so strong that I had to excuse myself immediately and talk with Jesus. Afterwards, I was sure it was a real call from God. When my husband came home, I told him what had happened to me.

The day finally came to meet the Foreign Missions Board. Even though I had definitely felt the call, I was elated when the board turned us down, telling us to go home and study the language. Needless to say, my husband did not have the same feelings, so I tried to feel unhappy too.

Back home, my husband went to the university and received his minor in Norwegian. He finally persuaded me to begin studying some Norwegian also, but it was more difficult for me, being a busy mother and, more important, not so excited about the idea. By this time, the church had grown to support us full time, and we sent a group from our church to begin another church forty miles away. This group included many of my relatives who had been saved. After this, I was rooted in North Dakota and pleased with everything. I also felt Brother Nilsen was finally satisfied. This was going to be our home.

Then he did it to me again. He said, "It is time to reapply to go to Norway." This time I knew it was right and did not argue. I only went to my knees and asked Jesus to help me to accept all the things that now would be coming my way.

A definite peace came over me, and I knew that everything would work out. I can't say that everything went smoothly all the time. When we had our garage sale and I saw all my things going, when we left our house for the last time and I stopped to look and feel my brand-new carpet, I must admit I shed some tears. When I said good-bye to my family and friends, I thought I would break into pieces. But when I look back on two missionary terms (including deputational travel), I wouldn't change the decision or refuse to go.

Has everything happened just as I would like for it to? No, certainly not! Just as there are heartaches and disappointments in the United States, so there are in any country. Nevertheless, I am thankful that I finally said yes. There is no strength in me alone, but God has given me the strength and peace and joy that only He can give, circumstances notwithstanding.

We eventually also went to Sweden, but that is another chapter. I regret nothing I have given to the Lord.

The will of God has brought Sister Nilsen full circle and has returned her to the United States. Presently, the Nilsens are pastoring in Moorhead, Minnesota. Both daughters are now married, and their son is still at home helping Mom and Dad.

But what think ye? A certain man had two sons; and he came to the first, and said, Son, go work to day in my vineyard. He answered and said, I will not: but afterward he repented, and went. And he came to the second, and said likewise. And he answered and said, I go, sir: and went not. Whether of them twain did the will of his father? They say unto him, The first . . . (Matthew 21:28-31).

The storefront church in Stockholm, Sweden.

Corliss Nilsen and family in Stockholm, Sweden, November 1988.

CHAPTER 10

Theresa DeMerchant

BRAZIL

I was born on a farm in Custer, Wisconsin, to a family of nine. We were Catholics. One day, when I was five years old, a Watkins dealer from Clintonville, which was sixty-five miles away, came to our home to sell some of his household products. He invited my mother and aunt to a product display in his home in Iola, about thirty-five miles from our home. While my mom and aunt were in his home, his wife invited them to a church meeting at their house on Sunday afternoon. At this house meeting, my parents were converted.

The closest United Pentecostal Church was in Clintonville. We had an old 1935 Chevrolet and could only make it to church about once a month since the roads were so bad due to the snow. In spite of these circumstances, I received the Holy Ghost when I was eight and was baptized in Jesus' name at age nine. An attempt was made to start a church in our town, but unfortunately, it closed in just a short time.

I always adored the piano player in Clintonville, who is now Ruth Munsey. Her mother was the Sunday school teacher of my junior class. One day she asked how many would like to be a pastor or a pastor's wife. I quickly raised my hand.

I was not able to go to church regularly, due to the distance and the difficulties. However, I read my Bible, prayed regularly, and prepared myself for the work of God. When I was twelve, I baby-sat in order to pay for local piano lessons, which I took for eight years. I also played the accordion, sang, and helped in Sunday school.

When I was seventeen, I spent several weeks in prayer and received a refreshing of the Holy Ghost. I would go to prayer meetings at an Assemblies of God church in town, since we had no local United Pentecostal Church. In my last year of high school, we moved to Madison, Wisconsin, where we finally had a local United Pentecostal Church. I prayed every chance I could for God's will in my life.

One day God clearly spoke to me and asked if I would be willing to go to a foreign field. I prayed more, wanting to know where. After some weeks, God spoke "Brazil" to me. He gave me such an intense burden for Brazil that I cried at night. Every time I prayed, I had to pray for Brazil first. The only thing I knew about the country was what I had seen on some slides at a youth camp when I was twelve. I remembered seeing the beautiful green forests and jungles and thinking, If I am ever a missionary, this is where I'd like to go.

After more prayer, in 1954 I decided to go to the Apostolic Bible Institute (ABI) in St. Paul, Minnesota. I intended to prepare to be a missionary to Brazil.

After I graduated, I still didn't feel any closer to my goal. S. G. Norris, the Bible college president, asked me to stay at ABI to teach piano lessons and English, since they were my best subjects. He also asked me to be his secretary. I agreed.

I attended Macalester College during the summers, studying Spanish among my other courses, since I thought it would help me with Portuguese, the language spoken in Brazil.

I taught at ABI for two years, but none of the fellows I dated wanted to be a missionary. In 1959, a Canadian, Bennie DeMerchant, arrived at ABI. I didn't consider him quite grown up since he was only eighteen and very, very thin. After all, I was twenty-three. Soon after he arrived, he gave a testimony in church saying he wanted to be a missionary to Brazil. I poked my roommate and playfully said, "Maybe he'll be my husband." Actually, he was so young and so pitifully thin that I could hardly imagine it.

Little did I know that he was planning to ask me out on his first date-night in February. The rules were that you had to be a second-semester student before you were allowed to date. He now tells the story that one day he bought some gum out of a machine while I was waiting in line behind him to buy some also. He turned and asked me if I would like a stick of his gum. He now says, "That was the most expensive stick of gum I've ever bought in my life."

Our first date was spent in his car spinning circles on the ice. I was scared to death that the doors would fly open, and I would fall out. (As I said, he was very young.) Nevertheless, on July 22, 1961, we were married in the church chapel at ABI. Anyone who knows my husband will not be surprised to learn that our honeymoon was spent fishing in Canada. Might I add that this was my first and last fishing trip. Wading waist deep in icy water is not my cup of tea.

He graduated in 1962, and we took a country church one week later in River de Chute, New Brunswick, Canada, where we pastored for a year. There was no indoor water and only outdoor facilities. We had to rough it, but being a farm girl, I didn't mind. Besides, wherever my husband was, that is where I wanted to be.

We dreamed of the time we could be missionaries. We could hardly wait for the chance to meet the Foreign Missions Board. We met with them but were turned down and told to wait because Bennie was only twenty-two years old.

In 1964—only one year older—we met the board again. Before the meeting, the Lord gave us a verse of Scripture: "So send I you." We were appointed! When Brother Box, the secretary of foreign missions, told us the good news, we were so happy that we felt like hugging each other.

Brother DeMerchant was ordained at the conference on the same day we were commissioned. What a day! That same month I had learned that I was pregnant after having been married for three years. All our prayers were answered at once!

At the time we were appointed, we were assisting Brother Rolston in Plaster Rock, New Brunswick, Canada, and I was teaching music in the public school. After six months, I quit teaching, and we traveled to Ontario, Texas, Wisconsin, Louisiana, and several other places as we received invitations from various pastors. There was no Partners in Missions program at that time, but many kind people offered their assistance.

Years earlier, my husband had a vision of the Amazon, so he chose the capital city of Manaus for us to live in. As long as it was in Brazil, I was happy. When our first child, Beth, was six months old, we flew to Manaus. I was so happy; it had been twelve years since I had first felt my call to Brazil.

Our parents were very saddened at our leaving, and of course, their sorrow hurt us. However, we were still happy, laughing, and ready for any challenge. I did have fearful reservations of bringing my little baby to a place where I knew nothing of the medical care or the hygiene, but I knew God had called and He was able to see us through anything. We didn't have furniture or a home to leave behind, so we had nothing to give up.

Over the years, our biggest concern has been for our children. In spite of problems, including culture shock for our children when they returned to the United States, God has always helped us. Beth, our older daughter, is happily married to a young minister. They had a precious baby boy whom God took only a few weeks after his birth. We were all devastated by the loss, but the Lord then gave them a beautiful little girl who is the delight of our life. Our daughter Pamela graduated from ABI and is now doing well and attending church in Houston, Texas. We are thankful for her strength and dedication.

On June 15, 1992, Bennie Jonas, our only son, went to be with the Lord at almost sixteen years of age. "He hath delivered his soul in peace from the battle that was against him" (Psalm 55:18).

Bennie Jo loved to fish and fly with his dad in the float plane in which they flew together to reach the interior jungle villages. He was a rowdy little fellow who grew to be a sincere Christian with strong, unwavering faith and the touch of God on his life to the end. His, and our, earthly desires for his future, for the kingdom of God, were shattered as he passed on after a long, brave fight of a year and a half with bone cancer.

During the last week he could only turn his head a little and barely move his right hand. He wrote in his diary, "I reminded myself that God would never leave me nor forsake me, and I felt God's joy in my heart. I want to be strong and of good courage. My body belongs to God. He can do what He wants with me. After all this, my neck is very heavy and my eyes are hurting."

On what was to be his last day, I was still in a guest room a few blocks away when I received a call to hurry to the hospital. We had been believing God for a miracle, so I ran all the way to the hospital laughing, because I was convinced that he had received his miracle. When I arrived, however, I learned that instead of receiving a miracle, he had received his promotion. God's will for Bennie Jo to leave us was accomplished. In spite of the traumatic blow and anguish, I knew God was with us and would give us the strength to somehow accept our almost overwhelming loss.

His dad had been with him and said about an hour before he finally left us he loudly shouted, "I'm healed, I'm healed! From head to toe, I'm healed!" He may have had a vision of his perfect spiritual body, or he may have been released from pain before being set free from the body. He had previously had a dream that he was kneeling down and kissing the streets of gold. Once when his dad was gone on deputational travel, Bennie Jo told me, "Tell Dad that there is going to be a great revival in Brazil." Isn't that what it is all about? In spite of our grief, God's will be done.

My husband continues to be the superintendent of the Amazon District as well as the president of the church in Brazil. God is faithful, and we have seen a great gathering of souls, for which I am truly thankful.

Our personal losses have pierced our soul, but in this present life we will all be tried with fire; being a missionary does not cause them nor does refusing a call mean we will escape them. As for the call of God to the foreign field, even after thirty years I wouldn't trade places with anyone. Being a missionary brings great joy and fulfillment in spite of many tribulations. Our greatest joy will be when we present thousands of Brazilian sheaves before the Lord. Again I say, "Thank God we came."

Beloved, think it not strange concerning the fiery trial which is to try you, as though some strange thing happened unto you: but rejoice, inasmuch as ye are partakers of Christ's sufferings; that, when his glory shall be revealed, ye may be glad also with exceeding joy (I Peter 4:12-13).

Theresa and Bennie DeMerchant, 1996.

Theresa DeMerchant and Melissa Anderson at a ladies conference in Brazil, 1993.

Theresa DeMerchant coaching Bible school student in Manaus, Brazil, 1994.

Theresa DeMerchant organizing the conference youth choir, 1994.

CHAPTER 11

Millie Scott

MADAGASCAR

It was a warm August day, and I was standing with my dad on the campgrounds at Newcastle Bridge, New Brunswick, Canada. I might have been six or even younger. I was still small enough to clutch the leg of my dad's pants as he stood talking to another Pentecostal man. The man looked at me and said to my dad, "That one's going to be your missionary." I shall never forget those words. I do not know when God placed the call to be a missionary in my heart, but I do know that I grew up knowing that I would someday be a missionary. That knowledge and that desire were ever there.

Born in Amherst, Nova Scotia, Canada, I was the third in a family of six children. When I was two, I became ill with pneumonia and measles. The doctor said that by morning I would be either dead or completely deaf. Instead of crying by my bedside, Dad went to church and had the church pray for me. God performed a miracle and proved the doctor wrong.

At the age of seven I was hospitalized, and after tests were run, the doctor concluded that I had a bone disease in both my heels. For three months, I wore casts from my knees to my toes. I missed sixty-three school days that year. After getting the casts off, for several years I wore shoes with built-up heels. Dad would often have me prayed for. I do not know whether God healed me or it was something I outgrew, but my heels became fine with not a trace of any problems.

The greatest miracle of my life happened on August 18, 1959, when I repented of my sins, and on August 19, when I was filled with the Holy Ghost at the age of twelve. Around one o'clock in the morning people half-carried me to the car because I was so drunk in the Spirit I couldn't walk straight. I would wake up in the night talking in tongues. From that time the awareness of the call to be a missionary was very strong in my life.

The slides or films that missionaries would show in our church would affect me so. My heart would yearn within me. Each of my decisions, such as what courses to take in high school or what boys to date, was based on how it would affect my future work for God as a missionary. In grade ten I began to pray to know God's will after I graduated. Should I become a teacher, go to Bible college, or go straight to work in an office? My dad was a salesman and a hardworking man, but there never was enough money. I did not feel that I could ask my dad for money for my Bible college bill.

In twelfth grade God showed me that I should not be a teacher. He also let me know that I should go to Bible college but that it was all right for me to work to get some money first. Since I had taken courses in high school to prepare me for office work, I was able to get good jobs right after graduation. God gave me these jobs, because experienced girls were looking for work and couldn't find any, yet I walked off the street and got one.

I worked at my first job for seven months, and then I got a call from the personnel department of our provincial government offering me a job as a civil servant in one of the provincial divisions. Of course I took it. I used to think that I was one of God's pets because He was always doing special things for me, and He still is!

During these two years of working I didn't get away from the mission call. No way! I was saving money to pay my Bible college bill.

Somehow God let me know the time that I should start Bible college. His timing is always right. I did not know that would be the year a young man would start Bible college and receive his missionary call in his second year of school. Neither did I know that God had chosen me to be his wife, but God knew! And so He led me and guided me because I sought Him, loved Him, and was excited about serving Him.

The enemy will try to stop us from doing God's will if he can. Just before Bible college started, the devil put doubts in my mind. I had been accepted and had already bought black skirts and white blouses for school. We had to wear them when we went out to minister in the churches on weekends, and weekend ministry was part of our training. I had purchased the other things I needed for school and was excited about going in a few weeks. One weekend I went home to visit my parents, and since there were special services in our church, I went to service on Friday evening.

All during the preaching doubts came to my mind such as, "The only reason you're going to Bible college is to get a man." (That is what one lady had said to me, and I told her that God knew it wasn't true. But if I got one, I wouldn't complain.) Then the enemy would say, "What if it isn't God's will?" That night I went home, knelt by my bed, and told God that for years I believed He was calling me to Bible college and that I was going unless He shut the door. Peace came to my heart, and I forgot all about the doubts.

The next night I went back to church, and after the evangelist preached, he called all the young people up to the front. He came over to me and told me God had His hand on my life. He said, "I don't know what was going on between you and God last night, but while I was preaching I saw a cloud over your head. Whatever it was, you have settled it with God." To me that was a confirmation that I should go to Bible college to prepare to be the missionary God had called me to be.

While I was in my second year of Bible college, my mother needed an operation on her back. It was her second back operation, and she was in the hospital for several weeks. After returning home from the hospital, she still needed weeks of bed rest. I came home from school to look after the three younger kids—two sisters and a brother—while Mom had her operation and after she came home. I kept up with my schoolwork by going to the Bible college once a week, which was thirty miles away, and getting my work for the following week. I would write tests while I was there.

During this period of my mother's convalescence she came to depend heavily on me. After so many weeks I had to prepare to go back to Bible college for my third year. When I began to talk about leaving, Mom would weep, cling to me, and make me feel that I could not leave her. I felt as if I were trapped, as if I were in a cage. I could see my future crumbling. I knew that if I didn't leave I would be looking after my mother (as well as my father and the kids) for years. I also knew that if I were to remain at home, my future as a missionary would be ruined.

It was a very difficult time. My mother would not have wanted that to happen, but the enemy tried to use this situation to hinder God's will in my life. I made the decision to go back to school. I felt as if this decision made me seem like a harsh, unloving daughter, but my mother got well, and we have had a good relationship. God will take care of things if we will follow Him.

Two years later, after marriage, my husband and I were pastoring his home church. I was on the front lawn of the little house we were renting, talking to God and telling Him that I loved Him. Then I realized that these were only words I was saying, and I asked God how I could prove to Him that I loved Him. He answered, "By working for me." I was a pastor's wife, but I longed to be a missionary's wife.

We were in home missions in Nova Scotia for seven years. At one point during that time, I asked the Lord if this work was the fulfillment of the mission call He had given me. But God is never in a hurry, and He had to prepare us and work with us to get us ready. Fourteen years after we graduated from Bible college, we were appointed as missionaries.

On November 27, 1984, as I walked off the plane in Madagascar, I saw some Malagasy people standing around, and tears came to my eyes. As I descended the steps of that plane I said, "God, these are my people. I've come home."

He that loveth father or mother more than me is not worthy of me: and he that loveth son or daughter more than me is not worthy of me (Matthew 10:37).

Preaching at ladies conference in Mauritius, 1995.

Teaching the wives at a 1989 preachers conference.

Teaching youth camp in 1993.

Speaking to ladies at a conference, November 1984.

CHAPTER 12

Bobbie Carpenter

SOUTH AFRICA, SWAZILAND, AND LESOTHO

Even though I was very young, as I began to speak with other tongues when the Holy Ghost filled my heart, I knew that one day I would go to a foreign field. The distinct call came about a year later when I was seventeen years of age. God strongly impressed upon my heart that I would preach and teach in a country in Africa where I would not only work with blacks but also with whites, Indians, and a mixed-race people.

This call was fulfilled when I reached the Republic of South Africa. In South Africa, thirty years ago, we had to work with each race separately, for this was required by the government of the country.

Mack Carpenter, who is now my husband, was a member of the same church. As a young man he, too, felt his call to Africa just after he received the Holy Ghost. Our pastor, knowing we both had received a call, put us to work, admonishing us, "You need all the experience you can get." We taught Sunday school, preached revivals for neighboring churches, held tent revivals, preached in the city jail and on the street corner, visited the sick, and taught Bible courses. Everything we did was first to please Him and second to prepare ourselves for our calling. All of this we did in the three years (1950-53) after we received the Holy Ghost and before we were married.

On Saturday, June 13, 1953, we were married. The next day, Sunday, June 14, we were in Flatwoods, Louisiana, beginning a brush-arbor revival meeting that lasted six months. Flatwoods was a small town that had no church. We were now home missionaries.

We remained in Flatwoods until May 1954. After seeing a church building erected and about seventy-five precious souls filled with the Holy Ghost, we left Louisiana to go a thousand miles north to the state of South Dakota. We met the S. R. Hanby family and helped bring in a work for the Lord in a state where there were no United Pentecostal churches. We went to the city of Sioux Falls and remained there for eleven years, founding the church that is there today. It was a cold country and hard work, but the Lord gave us souls! We gained experience that was good for us when we reached Africa.

During the eleven years in South Dakota, the Lord would not let either of us rest from our calling to Africa. We felt God wanted us to go to Liberia. He even placed a location called Klay on our hearts, which we had never heard of. Later we read in the *Pentecostal Herald* that a work was being established there, even though we ourselves did not get to go there.

We applied for Liberia six times during these eleven years, first while Wynn Stairs was the foreign missions director and later when Oscar Vouga was the director. We never made it to Liberia. We did not qualify for what the brethren of the board were looking for each time we applied. First, they needed a pilot . . . next teachers . . .

and on and on, until we began to wonder, What is wrong with us?

Never did we question our calling. We knew that in God's time we would reach Africa. The board even asked us to go to another field. Others have changed fields and it has been the will of God for them to do so, but we could not feel this was what *we* should do. Each time we were turned down, we went back to our home missions work and continued to pray, "God, Your will be done!" It was not easy.

Brother Vouga came to us after we were not passed for Liberia at the general conference of 1964 and said, "You keep wanting to go through the western door into Africa. That door is always closed, but the southern door is open. The Freemans are in need of help there. Will you go if you can get a visa?"

We agreed to go back to our room, pray, and let the board know our decision the following morning. We prayed almost all night. The following morning we told the board that we were willing to go to South Africa.

On March 16, 1966, we flew to Johannesburg, South Africa, as one of the happiest of families. We had now reached the land of our calling. We were surprised to find a country so beautiful, so civilized! We had prepared ourselves for jungles, headhunters, and the like. God was better to us than we deserved!

As home missionaries for eleven years, we did not have many material possessions. We reached our field of labor with our suitcases, Ladies Auxiliary appliances, linens (Louisiana ladies blessed us with these), and a few things that Sister Freeman advised us to bring with us to the field. There was no Partners in Missions program, but we believed God! Hadn't He already proven Himself to us on the home mission field?

We remained on the field for twenty-eight years until we felt our work was completed. Our health remained good, God supplied our needs, and we enjoyed being missionaries!

Our four children were eleven, nine, four, and three when we reached Africa. They have grown up in Africa. They received as good an education as they would have at home. They all received the Holy Ghost and were baptized in the name of Jesus. They are well-balanced, happy adults. They have their problems, of course, but none of them blame their problems on their being missionary kids. They love the Lord, and they loved Africa and missionary work. Our son is a missionary today.

We believe God has had His will in our lives. We give Him the glory for the work that has been done both in South Africa and Swaziland!

We would like to admonish the young couples starting out for the Lord in their respective fields. Believe in the Lord! Believe in His Word! If He called you, He will keep you! He will be with you! He does not lie, and His Word is sure! If you plant or water, He has promised to give the increase! May God bless you as you give your all to His service, in Jesus' name!

In 1996 the Carpenters were appointed to Lesotho and are continuing their work for the Lord in Africa.

Who can find a virtuous woman? For her price is far above rubies. The heart of her husband doth safely trust in her (Proverbs 31:10-11).

Bobbie Carpenter speaking at a ladies conference in South Africa.

CHAPTER 13

Beverly Tilley

NORWAY

I was born in a little place called Fort Scott, Kansas, to parents who were not Christians at the time. My father died when I was five, so I never really got to know him well. However, my mother always had a desire to serve the Lord.

I was about ten years old when I was first introduced to the Pentecostal experience. We were living in Houston, Texas, when my mother met a man who was a backslider. He told her what she needed to do in order to make herself and her children happy; he said she should start attending a United Pentecostal Sunday school. Then, one week some ladies from Pastor Fauss's church came to invite people to Sunday school. When asked, my mother said yes, she would like for us to attend. We went the next Sunday.

Although we liked it very much, we decided that it was

too far for us to walk. Instead, we began attending Pastor Dees's church where we could walk and attend on our own. At this church I first saw people receive the Holy Ghost, shouting with the joy of the experience.

My mother's sister would pick us up sometimes after Sunday school. She told my mother, "You are driving these children crazy, and you are going to be insane yourself if you don't stop attending that fanatical church." Most of my mother's family turned against her and said many critical things about the United Pentecostal Church; however, this never discouraged her. She knew that some Pentecostal people did not live up to the Bible standards and teaching, but that failed to discourage her from attending a church that did. She had found something real from God, and she wanted to continue in it the rest of her life.

We moved from Houston, Texas, to Louisiana to take care of my stepfather's sister. She was a wonderful saint of God. The very first Sunday in Louisiana, my mother received the Holy Ghost. This made such a change in our lives! She was baptized in Jesus' name on her birthday. I saw my mother happy for the first time in several years. Because of this, a desire was put in my heart, too, to serve the Lord.

I was ten years old when I started to school in Louisiana. This is where I met my husband. He was ten years old also. There was a kinship between us, because he was also Pentecostal and had been raised in a third-generation Pentecostal home. His mother received the Holy Ghost at age ten and has been living for the Lord for more than seventy years. That was completely different from my family, but I always looked at him as a great friend.

As I look back now, I can see there was a special bonding between us from the beginning, although we never became interested as a boyfriend or girlfriend until our senior year. Then we became engaged in April. In July, my husband-to-be and I went to the altar together. We dedicated ourselves to God, were filled with the Holy Ghost, and received a stronger determination to live for Him. In September, we started our married life living for God, which has always paid off. We have always enjoyed living for the Lord and putting Him first in our life.

My husband attended college during the first year of our marriage. He then took a secular job working for Exxon Oil Company in Baton Rouge, Louisiana. We attended a small church there and helped with the music.

My husband had received a call to the ministry when he was a teenager but had fought against it for years. He told me after we started dating that I might be marrying a preacher. At that time, it never dawned on me or even mattered that he was called, but when the Lord started dealing with him again, I began to realize the seriousness of it.

While we were in Baton Rouge, he made a decision to give his life completely over to the Lord and to do His work. Almost immediately we started pastoring a little home missions church. We were still very young.

Our daughter was two months old when we started pastoring, and during that year or the next my husband received his call to be a missionary. I loved missions and I loved souls, but missions was never that big in my life.

One night my husband had a dream. In the dream, he had a telephone call from his best friend. In the background he heard a black choir singing and said, "Oh, oh, my God, my God, it's Rhodesia." (The country is now called Zimbabwe.) In his dream he kept trying to talk to a missionary man but couldn't. All he could see was a lady, but he didn't talk to her. Instead he kept straining to talk to a man.

The next morning, the dream was on his mind so strongly that he told me about it. He said, "You know, I'm going to look on the map and see where Rhodesia is." We looked for it together, but I still didn't think very much about it. Then he said, "I'm going to look in our ministerial directory to see if we have a missionary there." When we opened the directory, we learned that there was indeed a missionary there, a lady named Wilma Ruth Nix.

He looked at me strangely and said, "That's why I could never talk to a man. We do not have a man there. I feel that God has called me to go to Rhodesia to work with those people."

This thought bothered me! In fact, it scared me to death. I thought, Oh, no, not Africa, not Africa. All I could think of was grass huts, the bush, and how strange things would be.

We talked a little bit about his feeling, but it was not yet a big issue in our lives. To him it was very serious, but he was just letting me follow along.

About two weeks after his dream, I decided to visit my mother. I took my daughter, and we stayed for three or four days. Then on a Wednesday night, as we were getting ready to go to church, my husband called and told me that he was going to resign from the church that night. He was doing this without my being there, which upset me very much. I requested prayer for him at Mom's church.

The next day, I went to my mother-in-law's home to stay with her until the weekend, and then my daughter and I were going to drive back home. When I entered her house, she greeted me and then said, "Do you know we are going to have a missionary here this next week?"

"Oh, you are?" I responded. "Who's that?"

She said, "I don't really know. I think its somebody like a Sister Nix."

I just stood there with my mouth open in shock. We didn't even know she was in the United States. We had never met her and never really expected to, and here she was going to be at our former home church. I finally said, "Whatever you do, do *not* tell Eddie." I told her of his dream and everything that had happened, and then I said, "He will want to come up here and talk to her, and I don't want this to happen. He can't afford to miss work." (We were in a home missions work, and he was having to work full time to make ends meet.) "He won't have the time or the money to come here to talk to her, so let's just keep this a secret."

That weekend my mother- and father-in-law went home with us. When we got home, my husband was out doing some church work so I reminded my mother-in-law, "Be sure and remember what I said, and be sure you do not tell him." It was like a joke with her, but I was serious.

My husband came in shortly after that, and in just a few minutes my mother-in-law said, "Now remember, we are not going to tell him."

Of course, he asked, "Tell me what?"

I said, "Oh, Ma Tilley, you shouldn't have *said* that!"

He asked, "Tell me what? Tell me what?"

I replied, "Sister Nix is going to be at their church next week."

He said, "I'm going!"

I said, "I told you, Ma Tilley." Then I suggested, "Honey, listen. Why don't you first call the missions man, find out where she is, call her, and talk to her on the phone."

He took my advice and found that she was at a church just up the road. Naturally! Immediately Sister Nix wanted to talk to us. I was in the living room and he was in the kitchen on the telephone talking to her when I heard him start to cry. I could even hear her crying on the other end. I started to walk past him to go into the bedroom, when the Spirit of God hit me like a bolt of lightning, and we began to speak in other tongues.

Sister Nix said, "I know this is confirming your call to the mission field."

My husband answered, "I want to come meet you."

She replied, "No, I want to come to your home to meet you."

We arranged for her to come to our church to have a

missions service. When the time came for the service, she drove three hundred miles to be with us and talk to us. She repeated, "It is the will of God. I know it is the will of God for you to be missionaries." She then advised us to go to Texas Bible College and to absorb all we could about the school, for it was her desire to have a Bible school in Rhodesia. If the Lord was willing, she wanted us to work with her there.

We had already resigned our church, which obviously proved to be the will of God. We left in January to attend Bible college. My husband sent in an application to the Foreign Missions Division, but being very impatient he called about two weeks later to learn if it had been processed and when he was to meet the board. The answer we got was, "Stay in Bible college and learn all you can. You are young and have plenty of time."

This answer was very discouraging to my husband. Finally he asked, "Are we going or not?" We didn't realize then the time required to process our application and meet the board. He became more impatient. Eventually he became so discouraged that we withdrew from Bible college and took an assistant pastorate close to New Orleans. The burden for missions never left. He only became discouraged and was in a learning process.

We assisted in a couple of other works and then built a work in Ville Platte, Louisiana. Although we built up the church, my husband never, for a moment, lost his desire to go to the mission field.

He told me one day, "The Lord is dealing with me about missions, and I am going to apply again, because I feel it so strongly." At that time, there was war in Rhodesia. "The Lord has told me, 'If there is any problem getting into Rhodesia, apply to go to Norway.'"

When we applied for Rhodesia, we received a letter in reply stating that because of the war there, it was proba-ble that we would not be able to get into the country. However, that didn't discourage us, as the Lord had already prepared us for the next step. My husband wrote and asked about Norway. We received a letter asking us to meet the board at the general conference in Indianapolis.

The Scandinavians needed missionaries badly. There was only Brother Johnson in Sweden, and he was getting ready to come home. When we met the board in Indianapolis, we were approved to go to Norway. Although we had never actually met with them before or been turned down, our previous experiences were a learning process and a time of growth.

I never had a direct call, but the Lord confirmed my husband's call to missions through Sister Nix and the experience we had during the telephone conversation with her.

For me, the step into the ministry was going to pastor the little home missions church. I had to give up my nice home and move everything into a trailer house. Then, we moved all over the country. Because of this, when we got ready to go to the mission field, it never crossed my mind that I would have a problem giving up anything. I also didn't encounter the problem of separation from my family, because I already had done that and adjusted to it. Nor did I worry about taking my daughter to Norway. I didn't know much about the country, but I did know that I was half Norwegian. My mother is a full-blooded Norwegian-American, so I knew the people would look more or less like us. By now, I had been through enough and grown enough so that none of these things really bothered me. I just wanted to go with my husband. I knew he had the call of God; therefore, I could trust him. Even more importantly, I trusted that the Lord would take care of us.

I knew that Norway was a cold country and that it would be very different. Because of my young age, I felt that I could learn the language. None of these aspects really worried me, because it was my trust in the Lord that had ultimately caused me to say, "Yes, Lord, I'll go. Whatever."

We have now been on the foreign field over nineteen years. Raising our children in Norway has been a most positive experience. Because it is very modern, it is a great country in which to raise children. Since it is not like many Third World countries, I can't relate to some of the problems faced there. But I am confident that the Lord would have enabled me to be willing to go to Africa, had the door been opened.

My son was born in Norway, and it was one of the greatest experiences of my life. We look forward to continuing to work in Norway, although we have had to leave our married daughter and grandbaby behind. In spite of how very much we love and miss them, I know that the Lord will continue to be faithful to my family. I'm very happy that one day I finally said, "Yes, Jesus, I will go."

He that findeth his life shall lose it: and he that loseth his life for my sake shall find it (Matthew 10:39).

Beverly, Eddie, and Shane Tilley in Norway, 1997.

CHAPTER 14

Becky Buckland

PHILIPPINES, CZECH REPUBLIC, AND SLOVAKIA

I am always so amazed to see how God works. And believe me, sometimes it does seem to be in mysterious ways!

Neither my husband nor I was privileged to be raised in a minister's home. My husband was reared in the Bible Church in Indianapolis, Indiana, since he was a year old. James Simison was a jewel of a pastor, principled, and a lover of God's Word. Growing up in such an atmosphere had a positive effect on my husband's life. When Brother Simison preached, he placed a deep desire in people to be the best they could be, convincing them that pleasing God was the most wonderful thing they could ever do.

I received the Holy Ghost at age eleven at the Illinois youth camp. My family came one by one into the Brookfield church, pastored by Eugene Erwin. I was so thankful when my dad received the Holy Ghost while I was attending Bible college in St. Paul, Minnesota.

Missionary services at our church were always a highlight. When I was a child, listening to their stories and seeing the pictures from faraway countries would always leave such an impression on me. I remember missionary services in the Brookfield United Pentecostal Church that took place nearly twenty-three years ago! These special, select men and women of God had the respect of all of us. No doubt about it, they were spiritual giants. How could anyone *want* to leave the good old United States and go to a place so strange that they eat ants?

Following high school graduation I went directly to Bible college. It was a wonderful experience for me. I was overwhelmed with all of the young people my own age who had come to study. I did a lot of growing up in those three years. There I met my husband-to-be, Roger Dale Buckland. Some people criticize young people for going to Bible college only for the intention of getting married. I don't know how many actually come for that purpose alone, but college age is the normal age for marriage, Bible college or no Bible college.

I am so thankful for the young man I met there. He changed my life permanently, and I do mean permanently! When he asked me to marry him, he said, "If you marry me, I promise we will go places." I thought I understood what he was trying to say. Has he ever taken me places!

We married soon after graduation in 1975 with our hearts agreed that we wanted to give God everything we had. We were both still very young, my husband being the ripe old age of twenty-one and I barely twenty years old. However, it was our desire to work in the ministry, even though we did not fully realize the total responsibility of it. Isn't God good to take us only one step at a time? If God had shown me what I would be experiencing in the future and where He was going to lead me, I probably would have fainted on the spot!

But our God is faithful and mindful of us. We both needed to mature and to learn many things before we would be totally on our own. Our first step, and quite an opportunity for us, was to become full-time assistant to the pastor and youth minister at Portage, Indiana, under Pastor Robert E. Henson. Neither of us had worked so close to church administration and leadership before. Watching Brother and Sister Henson work was a very good example to us. We are thankful for the two years that the Lord allowed us to have there.

Our next step was to begin full-time evangelistic work. Much could be said on how this ministry taught us so many things. Learning to live by faith is always a good experience, even when it hurts! For two years we went from church to church, singing (or trying to), preaching, and praying at the altar with new ones.

At the birth of our first son, Matthew, in 1979, we took the pastorate of the Apostolic Gospel Church in Ironton, Ohio. Here was where we settled in and had our first home, a second precious baby boy, Jonathan, and a lovely congregation. We thought we would be there until the Lord came back. It was not long before we were busy in the district. My husband became youth secretary for the state of Ohio. We kept working with a youthful zeal and saw the Lord do many things in our five years there.

Missionaries came and went through our church on a regular basis. With each one, our hearts would go out to them. I remember in particular George Shalm coming to our home. As we stood on our front porch saying our good-byes and thanks for coming, my eyes filled with tears. Again, the feeling of being in the presence of a spiritual giant overwhelmed me. As he pulled away, we prayed that God would be with him and bless him mightily. What a difference the ministry of this man made in India!

The Lord has a plan for all of us. In His own time He takes each of us in His hands and works with us to prepare us. The Lord must have thought we were almost ready for what He had in mind for us, because the next missionary to visit our church was Gordon Mallory from the Philippines. Again, our spirits were as one as we talked and had fellowship. Brother Mallory looked at my husband and asked if we would be interested in preaching two youth camps in the Philippines.

Interested? Did he realize what he just asked us? The two of us, being shoulder to shoulder on a foreign field with our missionaries? What an experience of a lifetime! We made every sacrifice necessary and made that trip. It was the trip that changed our lives.

After returning from this fantastic experience, every time we prayed our hearts would ache for the Philippines. We could see the faces of the people and hear their voices. It was not long before our application was before the Foreign Missions Board. After all the processing was completed, we were appointed in October 1984. We resigned our lovely church, sold our home, and headed on our first deputational trip with a five-year-old and a three-year-old son.

We were one happy family when we finally arrived in Manila in April 1986. We found a home to rent in Davao City, Mindanao Island, and settled in. Our faith was high, and we were ready to do a great and marvelous work!

Carl Varnell had arranged a nine-day trip for my husband to many different areas of Mindanao to introduce him to the work and the ministers we would be working with. He was so excited to go, and I was excited for him! I told him, "This is your very first missionary trip! Go get 'em!" It would be impossible to contact him while he was gone. We were on our own.

Little did I realize, but God was getting ready to help me climb up another step in Him. My husband had the car packed and ready to go, gave me a quick kiss, asked me to pray for him, and was soon out of the driveway. There I was, with my two small sons, Matthew at six years and Jonathan at four. We had only arrived weeks ago. This

was to be my first experience of being alone on the foreign field for a period of nine days with the boys. But I
was tough, I thought. We would be just fine. I knew that
God was using my husband. I wanted him to be proud of
us when he returned.

The church in Davao was having a revival, so I
thought it would be good if the boys and I went to show
support. We had no vehicle of our own to take, so we took
a bus. This was a new adventure for the three of us. We
got on the bus and proceeded to the church. The first
thing we noticed was that the windows of the bus had no
glass in them. The faster the bus went, the more dust and
dirt poured in. Two men were welding an old bicycle
beside the road. The white flashes of sparks flying everywhere in the night air caught my attention. These men
were not using the safety glasses I had seen in the United
States.

Here was God's first test for me. I did not know it at
the time, but a piece of that welding flew up through the
bus window and lodged in Jonathan's eye. He complained
that his eye hurt and kept rubbing at it. I thought it was
from all the dust and dirt on the bus ride. By the time we
returned home, all of us were filthy as the grime stuck to
our sweaty faces. I knew I felt dirty, so I washed him up
really good and put the boys to sleep for the night.

The next morning when Jonathan awoke, he could not
even open his eye. It hurt him so badly that he began to
cry. I then knew that something had happened. Perhaps he
got an infection in it from all of the dirt, so I thought I
would try to locate a doctor. We had just arrived in the
country, I did not know the Cebuano dialect, and I had no
vehicle, so where was I to start for help? There were
armed guards up and down the streets of our village, so I
went to them first. Through elementary attempts at trying
to make myself understood, and with the guard's response
of flying hands and unintelligible words, I found out that a
"doctora" (female doctor) lived nearby. Knocking on her

door, I was so relieved to find out that she understood English. She followed me to my house and looked at Jonathan's eye. He would have to go to the hospital for a further examination.

I left Matthew with a young girl from the church and headed out to the hospital with the doctora and my four-year-old son, Jonathan. My heart plummeted when I realized that the building we were pulling up to was considered the best hospital in the city. We walked through the wide-open doors into the dark corridors. Just like the bus, the windows had no glass in them; however, these windows had iron bars embedded in them. Dust was filtering in with every passing car. We could smell the exhaust of jeepneys and buses as they roared down the busy city street. I took a second glance when I noticed two of the workers playing with a cat on their desktop. This was a hospital?

After the examination, I was told that Jonathan had a foreign object in his eye, which required immediate surgery. What was I to do? Oh, how I wished my husband were there! Should I let them cut on my son's eye? I could hardly understand the doctor's broken English. I knew Jonathan could not be in this condition until the return of my husband, so I signed the papers for surgery.

They began to put tubes down his nose. The room soon became crowded as the employees of the hospital wanted to see the young American boy. They all stood around just staring at him. The first tube they tried to place down his nose was too large. They told me they were sorry, but they would have to pull this one out and get a smaller one. And there went the process again. Jonathan was frantic and was screaming to go home. I didn't blame him. I tried to tell him that everything would be all right; all the while my insides were shaking.

I began to plead with God: "Please, please, please, Lord, tell my husband that something is wrong and send him home. I need him right now!" I remembered listening to Nona Freeman in missionary services and had visions of her marching across Africa doing many exploits. What kind of a missionary was I? A frightened one, for sure. I didn't quite measure up to my expectations of what Sister Freeman was, or of what I thought I should be.

We headed to the operating room with Jonathan still crying. The operating room was nothing more than a room closed off by a sheet pulled across a wire. During the surgery, hospital workers went in carrying bunches of bananas on their shoulders. What were they doing during the operation, eating bananas?

I leaned against the filthy wall out in the hallway. I had never felt so alone in all my life. There I was, a brand-new missionary, and I didn't know if I could take it or not. I prayed that they would not make a mistake on Jonathan's eye. I cried and then tried to regain my composure.

Our stay in the room is another story in itself. Finally, the surgery was over, and Jonathan and I were back home with Matthew before my husband came in from his trip.

I held up just fine in front of my sons, but as soon as my husband walked in the door, I fell on his shoulders and just sobbed.

God had been good. Twenty-three received the Holy Ghost on the trip. Now, I am thankful that God did not send my husband home. It was an important lesson for me. I had to learn to trust in Him, not in my husband. So many times we become frightened at what comes our way, but He is in the midst of it all. Many, many more times during our years in the Philippines I had to trust the Lord. And each time, it became easier and easier.

David said in the Psalms that his heart overwhelmed him. I have read the words he penned, "What time I am afraid, I will trust in thee" (Psalm 56:3). I have learned that we must not condemn ourselves for being afraid. Instead, we need to learn where to turn in our fear, as David did. We must place everything in God's care. There is a purpose to our hard times. With each passing test, our faith in Him becomes more solid. Psalm 119:71 says it so well: "It is good for me that I have been afflicted; that I might learn thy statutes."

The Bucklands did a tremendous job in the Philippines until they felt God leading them to go to Europe. They have recently begun a work in the former country of Czechoslovakia, which has been divided into the Czech Republic and Slovakia.

He hath made everything beautiful in his time (Ecclesiastes 3:11).

A sectional ladies conference on Mindanao Island. Some of the women dressed in their tribal clothing.

Sister Buckland and Sister Vergie Navallo (wife of Romy Navallo, now superintendent of the Philippines).

CHAPTER 15

Sandra Bracken

TAIWAN

I was privileged to be born into a home where precious, godly parents taught us the truths of God's Word. We were molded by their early morning prayers. Our sicknesses were healed when they called on God for us.

My early years of upbringing were in Idaho. In a small church there, I was only seven years old when the Lord began to speak to me about being a missionary. A missionary came to our church, and the wife stood to give her testimony. I and four other children in our family, who always sat on the front row, were listening to every word. We heard her tell how difficult it was for her to make the sacrifice to go with her husband overseas as a missionary. She talked about all the things she had to give up. My heart was deeply touched.

I had only had the Holy Ghost a few months at this time. I began to make a dedication in my heart to the Lord that night. I said, "Lord, if You call me to go to the mission field, You won't have to ask a second time."

From that time, the Lord began talking to me more and more. At the age of nine, we moved to Oregon to start a home missions work. When I was twelve years old, I felt God's clear direction to begin worship services during the noon hour at school. I carried my accordion to school every day, and I wrote personal invitations to each of the girls in my class to come to this time of worship. I told them that if they had any questions about the Bible, they could ask me, and if I didn't know the answer, I would ask my dad, who was a pastor, and come back with an answer the next day.

I tried to use every method to witness to others without being a nuisance. One of my teachers went to another church and would mention things now and then to let people know that he believed in God. One day I finished my assignment as quickly as possible so that I could ask him a question. I got my Bible, went to his desk, and asked, "Sir, can you explain Acts 2:38 to me? So many people there received the Holy Ghost that day. What does the Holy Ghost mean? Why were about three thousand baptized in the name of Jesus? Why was everyone in the Bible always baptized in the name of the Lord Jesus Christ, yet today people say it's incorrect?" He said he didn't have an answer, but he would think about it.

A couple of years later as I entered high school, I felt the Lord preparing me for the future. I tried every time I could to witness for the Lord. I helped start a Bible club that met after school every Wednesday. I invited different ministers in the area to speak.

One spring day during my junior year, something happened that had a great effect on my life. As I was studying in the library a voice said, "Go to the student council office and pick up an application to run for secretary of your high school."

At first, I thought it was only my own idea and that my flesh was trying to raise itself up to be honored by the other students. I was not willing that my flesh should have this kind of glory, so I began to rebuke myself: "What are you trying to do? Who do you think you are?" I ignored the thought and continued to study. But then the voice came to me again and again. I tried to brush it off, but the third time I stopped and asked, "Lord, are You trying to talk to me?"

Immediately I heard His response saying, "Yes, I want you to do this for Me."

I asked, "Lord, why do You want me to do this?"

He answered, "I want you to witness for Me."

With much trembling, I went to the student council office to pick up an application. Within a couple of hours I had the necessary twenty or thirty students' signatures along with five or six teachers' signatures to put me on the ballot. I took the application into the office to turn it in that day.

The principal said, "Sandy, may I see your student body card, please?"

"Oh, I don't have a student body card," I replied. A student body card was only used to get into sports games or dances. Since I didn't attend either one, I figured it wasn't worth the six dollars it cost. The principal then told me that without one I couldn't run for secretary.

That night as I knelt by my bed in prayer I told the Lord, "I guess You were only putting me through a test. I can't run for secretary of the student body because I don't have the money."

The Lord spoke, "You have a ten-dollar bill in your dresser drawer. Tomorrow, take it to school, buy a student body card, and then turn in the application."

The next day I did as God had instructed. When I returned home, I fell by my bed and prayed, "Lord, now You've gotten me into this, and I don't know what I'm going to say. I have no idea what to tell these people." Then I picked up my notebook and pen and said, "OK, Lord, I'm waiting for You to tell me what to say." The Lord began to pour words into my mind concerning what He wanted me to communicate to the students.

The day for the speeches arrived. We candidates were lined up on the platform waiting our turn to make a speech as to why we thought they should vote for us. I was afraid. Standing in front of the entire student body was considerably different from speaking to a few friends. I prayed, "Lord, if I stand up there and stutter and stumble while trembling with fear, it will give You no glory and You will receive no honor. I am asking You for a miracle because You see my fearful state. Bring peace to my heart and let me speak with boldness for You." When my name was called, the presence of the Lord came upon me like a blanket upon my shoulders. Peace covered me as I walked to the podium.

I began, "We live in a plastic generation. Many things you cannot trust anymore." I mentioned that many friends and even relatives are not trustworthy, but Someone *is* trustworthy and will stand close by you and never let you down. "His name is Jesus." I told the students that I was raised in a Christian home, but my parents had not forced me to live for God. It was my own choice, because I had learned that the Lord is my dearest friend. I added at the end, "If you would like for me to be your student body secretary, then vote for me."

As I returned to my seat, I was amazed at the applause from the entire student body. There was not one jeer or whistle, and no one laughed. The applause was respectful. After dismissal a young man from another school told me how surprised he was that I had the nerve to say what I did. He said the students in his school would have thrown things at the speaker. I told him, "Do you think the young people in this city are any different from the young people in your city? What I spoke today is what the Lord told me to speak, and He protected me. All the glory goes to Him!"

The students did elect me, and I became involved on other committees, putting me in contact with people I would not have been able to witness to otherwise.

At the end of high school, I went to Bible college. Again, the Lord was preparing me for the future. I tried to keep my heart in a condition that He could talk to me. I had several determinations in mind during this time. One that I did not mention to anyone at school, was to marry a preacher or not to marry at all. I knew the Lord was calling me to the mission field. I had prayed as a young girl, "Lord, don't give me a life of ease; help me work for You somewhere. Let me win souls for You. I don't care to make money or any of that. I just want to be involved in Your work."

At the end of the first year of Bible college, a young man in our class sold his car and bought a ticket to the Philippine Islands to work as a missionary helper for the summer. That sacrifice got my attention. I was thrilled when he wrote me a letter from the Philippines. To make a long story short, we were married one year later.

Right before our senior year, when Tom Bracken proposed to me, he told me that, first of all, his was going to be a life in the ministry—probably somewhere on a foreign field. It would not be a life of ease. Was that not what I had prayed as a young girl? Tom did not know that. He told me that it was possible that we would never have a home of our own, but that our life would be given to the work of the Lord. A chord of music in my heart that I had longed to play, seemed to sing forth that day as I saw God's hand on my life.

At the end of our senior year, I graduated side by side with my husband. We had already been invited to Napa, California, to intern under Paul Price, the Western District superintendent. We were blessed and honored of the Lord to have such a wonderful opportunity to work with Brother Price. Upon completion of our internship, the church gave us a lovely gift of luggage. Was that a hint? Actually, Brother Price asked us to stay and work with him while waiting for the Lord to direct our lives. He knew of our desire to work in the missionary field. While there, we learned many things that I hold dear to my heart.

After about three more years of training, we began to feel the time had come for us to leave Napa, although we dearly loved Brother and Sister Price and our friends there. One day Tom became desperate for clear direction and said, "I am going down to the church. I'm not coming back until I have direction from the Lord. I don't know when you can expect me back, but just pray for me. The Lord is going to give me direction, or I will just stay down there."

He went to the church and crawled up into the attic where no one would know where he was or interrupt him. He began asking God for direction. That evening when he came home I saw by the look on his face that God had given him an answer. We sat down to talk, but before he told me where God wanted us to go, the Lord was already speaking in my heart, "Taiwan—the Chinese people."

As he began to tell me about his vision and that God was calling us to the Chinese people, I was so excited in my spirit that God was giving us such clear direction. He was definitely calling us into His work with the Chinese people. It is difficult to express all the feelings in my heart, but I do feel honored by the King of kings to be able to serve among the precious Chinese people in Taiwan. During the eighteen years that we have been here they have become my people, but in turn it has been such a deep joy to see them embrace my God, to see them being filled with His Spirit, and to watch as they are baptized in His name, Jesus.

Several times one of the young ladies has come to me and hugged me while saying, "Sister Bracken, thank you for coming to Taiwan with the gospel!"

It is a joy, and to God be the glory.

My flesh and my heart faileth: but God is the strength of my heart, and my portion for ever (Psalm 73:26).

CHAPTER 16

Jeanne Norris

BRAZIL

I was raised in Spencer, Iowa, in a family of modest means financially but rich in the truth of God's Word, which was diligently taught to me. Even though my parents were Christians, I never had the slightest intention of being a minister's wife—much less the wife of a missionary. My plans for the future had been laid at an early age. They included marrying someone who would live close to my parents. We would have a lovely home and lovely children. I was part of a very close family, and the idea of leaving them was simply unthinkable.

At the age of eighteen, I met and married Robert Norris and began to live the life of my dreams. About three years after our marriage, my husband felt that he should attend Bible college. Although it was difficult to move away even this short distance, we sold the few possessions we had managed to accumulate and went to

Apostolic Bible Institute in St. Paul, Minnesota. Since I already had a two-year-old baby girl, I did not take any classes.

After one year of Bible college, my husband felt that he should actively enter the ministry. Naturally, I wanted to return to Spencer, Iowa, but we began to pastor a small country church in Kettle River, Minnesota. We pastored there awhile, then moved onto various other places to help out in short-time pastorates.

We had been pastoring six years in Clintonville, Wisconsin, when my husband told me that God had called him to go to Brazil. He planned to meet the Foreign Missions Board in the coming fall to get the ball rolling. My feelings at that moment would be hard to describe, since they were all in a jumble. A thousand things flew through my mind at once. Naturally I wanted to please God, but was *this* necessary? What about my beloved, elderly parents? With their health conditions, could they possibly survive until I returned?

My children! By this time, my oldest daughter was married with two children. Another daughter was seventeen. Our oldest son was eight years old, and the youngest was a baby boy of fourteen months. How could I leave my precious daughter and beloved grandchildren? How would my teenage daughter adjust? Who would be my little ones' playmates? What would the hygienic conditions and medical care be like? What type of food would I have to feed my family? Where exactly was Brazil, what language did the people speak, and could I possibly learn another language at my age?

I had a million doubts, confusions, and fears, but one thing I did know for sure: if my husband felt that God wanted him to go to Brazil, then any resistance from me would be a total waste of time and energy. Therefore, I quietly began to pray earnestly for God to change his mind; I knew I could never do what was being asked of me.

However, the more I prayed for God to change my

husband, the more He began in His gentle way to change me. He made me realize that my place was by my husband's side and that to oppose his call would hinder my husband's ministry and would be contrary to the will of God. The change was not easy, and it did not happen overnight, but I did surrender my own will to the will of God. I began to give my husband the full support that he needed and deserved. I trusted the Lord to give me the courage I would need and to supply the needs of our family. Once I accepted my husband's call, even though God never dealt directly with me, I made up my mind to be flexible, adjust to whatever circumstances would bring, and make a happy home for my family, wherever God chose to put us.

At that time, people were rarely appointed immediately but were asked to return the following year or at some later date. Therefore, thinking that we would feel out the situation before informing my parents and upsetting them, I decided not to say a single word to them about it. After meeting the board, we were sitting and enjoying the conference with several members of my family when it was announced that we had been approved as missionaries to Brazil. My family nearly went into shock, and my mother and I were both in tears. We had no idea they were going to announce this decision at the conference. Everything moved so quickly! We were presented, and funds were raised for our travel within only a few days.

We resigned our church the following spring. During the summer, my husband traveled to raise more of the necessary funds. Although I had accepted to obey God's will and follow my husband, I was still heartbroken over leaving my parents in their poor state of health. It was understood that under no circumstances could we return to the United States in less than five years. I was afraid my mother or father would pass away while we were gone. I was not concerned about material possessions and was willing to live frugally, but, oh, my parents and my beloved daughter and grandchildren were tearing my heart out! Even though I was hurting so much, I tried to encourage my family to accept God's will. Separation of families is always painful. This was especially true of our close family. But, praise the Lord, my fears concerning my parents were unfounded, for they did live for me to be with them again.

Looking back after twenty-seven years on the field, I can honestly say that I am glad that God called us to be missionaries. Both our sons were raised on the field, and both were fully appointed as missionaries to Brazil. I now have a sense of fulfillment and contentment that can only come from being in God's will.

Brother Norris also served as the regional director of South America. The Norrises now reside in Minnesota. Brother Norris teaches at Apostolic Bible Institute in St. Paul, where he once was a student.

Give her of the fruit of her hands; and let her own works praise her in the gates (Proverbs 31:31).

Sister Jeanne Norris teaching in the Rio Bible school.

CHAPTER 17

Sandra Langham

LIBERIA

The following poem was written by Sister Langham in memory of her daughter who, at age twelve, was accidentally and fatally shot by a young friend while they were serving in Liberia. Brother and Sister Langham continue to serve God faithfully while ministering in the United States.

And let us not be weary in well doing; for in due season we shall reap, if we faint not (Galatians 6:9).

The Beautiful Harvest

Thank you, Lord, for this dream come true;
My ultimate dream I credit to You;
For only through You could it come to pass
That I visit Liberia, my love, at last.

While visiting that land, my eyes rather observing,
And this favor from You, I'm quite undeserving;
The memories were many as my feet touched the soil,
For fifteen years in that land I'd toiled.

The sowing of seed was not easy, You know;
We planted in soil, and You made it grow;
Walking through jungles far and wide,
Wading the waters and stemming the tide.

Raft sinking in river, our lives almost lost;
Too immature, never counting the cost;
In retrospect now, looking back I see,
All heartaches and sorrows were hidden from me.

A glimpse in the future would have dampened my zeal,
And I'd never have gone to this harvest field.
Oh, You are all wise and beauty indeed,
To send me with joy, bearing Your precious seed.

Considering us privileged to carry Your Word
To far-distant villages, good news, never heard;
With our hearts full of victory, life flooded with zeal,
You helped us sow seeds in this barren field.

Our young, restless hearts bursting vibrantly to see
A bountiful harvest for eternity;
We nurtured the plants with utmost care,
Divine ingredients their daily fare.

They're fully grown now and a beauty to see;
What greater reward could be given to me?
I now see great evidence from Your seed sown,
Though sowing it then, the results unknown.

The fruit of Your seed visible everywhere,
To these people, You'd sent us, with Your love to share.

Sacrifice? A thousand times no;
'Twas my greatest pleasure Your seed to sow.

In African soil, my daughter lies.
Question You? No, for You are wise.
My footsteps were heavy, I shed bitter tears,
As I stood by the grave of twenty-six years.

Vivid were memories flooding my soul;
A flashback of time, many thoughts unfold.
For my years past, I stood in this place
With a heart that was broken, tears drenching the face.

You sent me this Scripture, right out of the blue:
"I'll not leave you comfortless, I'll come to you."
Weeping uncontrollably, I lifted my eyes,
Silhouetted against background of azure blue skies.

And over her grave was a new arch of two palms;
Then flooding the soul, surged a peace and calm.
Their branches were waving against clear blue haze;
I said in my spirit, They're giving God praise.

Flashing through my mind as a pointed dart,
Illuminating the soul and calming the heart;
Just as He promised that He would do;
"I'll not leave you comfortless, I'll come to you."

Rising from the tomb, contemplating the years,
My heart waxed lighter; I dried the tears.
I offered praise there, greatly humbled to be
Viewing the harvest He'd given me.

To all pastors' wives,
Take courage. You too,
If not now, in the future
Your harvest you'll view.

I called upon the Lord in distress: the Lord answered me, and set me in a large place (Psalm 118:5).

Ready to go on a three-day village trip, 1957.

CHAPTER 18

Elizabeth Rose Andrade

PORTUGAL

by Rachel Hattabaugh

Elizabeth Andrade, my mother and friend, was born in East Providence, Rhode Island, into a Christian Pentecostal family. She was one of fourteen children, but eight of the children died young due to various diseases. In spite of the immeasurable heartache from the loss of her children, her mother continued to take the family to church and serve the Lord. Her father was a cook on a barge that was out to sea a great deal of the time.

When she was about eight years old, her father stayed home from the sea and began to sell from the back of his truck fresh fish and vegetables that they grew on their farm.

Her mother died when she was thirteen, and her father died when she was seventeen.

As a child she desired to be a missionary, but after her mom died she stopped attending church. After leaving the

Lord, she became very depressed and would often stand on a nearby bridge and consider suicide. Her grandmother finally convinced her, at age nineteen, to attend a Jesus Name Pentecostal church with her. There she was baptized in Jesus' name and received the wonderful gift of the Holy Ghost. She had been away from God for six years and was overjoyed to be back.

She met my father in this church, and they were married when she was twenty. Dad was a good Christian but not in the ministry. She assumed she would never be a missionary, as she had planned as a child. My father worked various occupations to support us, including on the railroad and sometimes on a boat. They were trying to help a new church to get started, and they moved, with the three of us children, into a garage in order to give almost all their salary to this new work. The plan was to build a very large house that all of the workers would share, plus a chapel.

When my mother was twenty-nine; my brother, John, nine; I, eight; and Naomi, five; my dad was killed in a tragic accident on a boat. Because my mom only received a very small amount from the accident and had no other income, the leaders of the group threw us out of the garage. The night we had to get out and drive to the next town. She was wondering what on earth she would do to take care of her three fatherless children, when we had a head-on collision with a hearse. Thankfully, none of us received any harm other than minor scratches. There was a body in the hearse, but it was not disturbed. Our car was totally wrecked, and we had to stay in a nearby motel that night. Somehow, she got a job, and we made it.

Others from the large house were later turned out when they were no longer "useful." Many became bitter and blamed God for the way they were so shamefully treated. Mom knew she needed Him and loved Him far too much to blame Him for the devil's work. She made up her mind to hold on even tighter.

Many years later she received a local minister's license and opened a church in New Bedford, Massachusetts, in a rented storefront, driving almost an hour to reach it. My brother, who was married by then, was a big help in cleaning, painting, and even playing the piano. She pastored there about a year while working in a garment factory to pay rent, heating, and other expenses for the church.

When all the children were married and gone and she no longer could draw Social Security for us, she worked at various other jobs besides the garment factory, such as working in a five-and-dime store, making salad at a factory, and cleaning house for other people. (For a while she was house mother and cook at the Pentecostal Bible Institute in Mississippi).

She stopped pastoring for several years and became a member in a United Pentecostal church. Because her daughter moved to California and wanted her near her, she moved there. She took a taxi one day to find a United Pentecostal church in Los Angeles. She witnessed to the driver, and as a result, he, his wife, and children all came to the Lord. Now he is a minister of the gospel. She later found work as a live-in housekeeper for a wealthy lady who was very kind and paid her well. Since her expenses were few, she was able to save a little money.

She came to Argentina to be with my husband, John, and me and stayed almost a year. Though she didn't speak Spanish, she began to learn and did quite well. Everyone in our churches loved her dearly.

During the 1976 general conference in Anaheim, California, an appeal was made for people to dedicate their lives to the Lord. God had placed a deep burden on Mom for the people of Portugal, whom she already felt were her people since she was of Portuguese descent on both sides of her family. However, she spoke no Portuguese and only a small amount of Spanish that she had learned during her brief stay with us in Argentina.

When the appeal was made, Mom went forward and volunteered for Portugal. The foreign missions personnel
were kind but did not encourage her to go, for Mom was
sixty-one years old. Nevertheless, she took her modest
savings and went on her own.

When she arrived, arrangements were made for her to
live with a young Portuguese family who had a small baby.
Brother Domingues, a missionary there at that time, left for
the United States only one week after her arrival. He had
complete confidence in Mom and left her and a Portuguese
member, Sister Concha, in charge of the church books.
Mother was also in charge of the services in two churches.
What an awesome responsibility for anyone, especially at
her age and having to depend on an interpreter!

While living with the Portuguese family, she scrubbed
floors, prepared meals, washed diapers, and studied the
language. After she was on the field, headquarters put her
on the Associates in Missions program and sent her one
hundred dollars a month, which really helped.

Sometime later, new missionaries, Brother and Sister
David Edwards, came. It was a profound relief when they
arrived and took the responsibility, and she could just
work under them. They were very kind to her and found
her an apartment, cleaned it, and got it all ready for her.
They stayed one term and then transferred to Germany.
The saints were sorry to see them leave, but none missed
them as she did; she was again alone and responsible for
the work!

Brothers Scism and McFarland went to Portugal and
asked her to return to America for travel and then return
to Portugal under full missionary appointment. After a
short time of deputational travel she returned and was so
happy to be with her beloved people again. Later, Brother
Domingues came to Portugal again and stayed several
more years. By then, Mom was speaking Portuguese well,
the responsibility was not new to her, and she was happy
in her work for the Lord.

When time for deputational travel came again, she had been in Portugal eleven years. When she came to the United States and took the required physical, the results never reached headquarters and she was not reappointed. Though she was in her seventies, she still wept many tears from a broken heart because she was not allowed to return to Portugal.

At age seventy-four, with two thousand dollars from headquarters and a large box full of tracts, she took a trip to the Cape Verde Islands. These islands are located in the North Atlantic Ocean 350 miles west of Africa. The people speak Portuguese, which was enough for Mom to feel she must reach them with the gospel.

My son Mark, who was twenty-three, went with her to help for a few days and make sure she was settled in before leaving her there. They landed on an island, but the airport was in an area that looked like a desert. She asked Mark, "Where on earth are we?" Because they had a very large box of tracts plus a small amount of luggage, Mark had to leave her there to find some place to eat. She kept herself occupied by passing out tracts to people in the airport. When Mark returned and she went to eat, he took over passing out the literature. They were finally able to catch a taxi, which was a pickup truck, to a port where they boarded a boat to go to another island. Here is the rest of the story in Mom's own words:

"When Mark and I got on the boat, there were so many animals and boxes that I wondered where they could possibly find room for people. I finally found a spot on a wooden bench near a corner where they had some baby pigs corralled. They were white and were the cutest little things. They didn't smell much because the water kept flying over the rails and soaking them. They were pink by the time the trip ended. Though the pigs didn't smell, the people throwing up over the edge sure did! I thought a few times that I was going to join them, but I didn't. The worst smell came from the chickens under my bench. Once, I noticed the pigs grunting and complaining of their discomfort and told them, 'Poor things, you sure are miserable, aren't you? Well, so am I!'

"It took us twelve hours to reach the other island. When we arrived, we learned that there would not be another boat for several days, so Mark had to take that one back in order to catch his plane back home. He certainly wasn't looking forward to another twelve hours on that boat, and even worse for him was having to leave me on the dock, but he had no choice.

"Someone told me of a woman nearby who would put me up for the night, so I took a taxi there. Her house was clean and the sheets were too, so I stayed. By the time I got to bed I was totally exhausted and slept like a log. When I awoke, my bed was absolutely black with ants, but I had not felt one on me all night.

"I left there the next morning and went to a hotel. It was old, not very clean, and full of flies. There also was no water in the bathroom. I asked for some and was brought a bucket of cold water. Oh, well! The bed was covered with only one sheet, and they brought me a very damp wall tapestry to use for a blanket. There was just no way to get warm on that cool night because even my sheet was damp. When my body heat dried out one spot, I was careful not to move from that one place all night, or I would have been back on a damp area again.

"The hotel had the only restaurant. When I went to eat and saw how filthy everything was, I didn't want to use their dishes. The only thing I saw to do was to volunteer to work in the kitchen. This way I could at least make sure my food and dishes were clean. The kitchen was small and dark, and it was difficult for me to even clean my things because they had no soap. However, the Lord kept His hand on me, and I never became sick even once on the entire trip.

"Each evening I would fold two hundred tracts, and I would pass them out the next day. I later went to another island. I knew there was a Nazarene church there, so I took a taxi to it. The pastor was very kind and helped me to get a room at a hotel. He would have had me stay with him, but he had a house full of guests.

"At this hotel there was a shower, but no water again, not even in the commode. The room was covered with cockroaches; the bed was covered with them. A nice young man from the church arranged for me to have some fruit, but I had to keep it well hidden from the roaches. I again was given a bucket of cold water, but since I needed to wash my hair, they relented and brought me a bucket of warm water also. After all the pigs, chickens, ants, flies, and roaches, I felt like I was experiencing the plagues of Egypt and wondered if the bucket of water would turn to blood.

"The hotel breakfast was only bread and coffee, but at least there was a restaurant nearby where I didn't have to do my own dishes. The young man who got my fruit for me, took a taxi with me to a small airport and helped me with my luggage. Of course, I gave him and his pastor some of my literature. I then took a small plane to another island.

"While on this island I ran out of money and went to the American Embassy to try to tell my daughter, Rachel, to send me some. I had left a signed check with her in case it was necessary for some reason. The people at the embassy were kind and helpful and loaned me money until I could receive some from home. I'm sure this is not standard practice, and I thank God for His help."

By the time I received my mother's call from the embassy, I was frantic with worry. She had been gone six weeks without a word. She was disappointed that she had only been able to reach three islands and passed out "only just more than a thousand tracts." That was when she was only seventy-four.

After her return to the United States, she remained active, keeping as busy as possible trying to help the local church in Arvin, California. We kept a close watch on her when we heard her worrying, "I only reached three islands. If only I could get back over there and pass out more tracts to the other seven. . . ." She did not know of any conversions due to her trip, but she knew that God sent her and that His Word would not come back void.

Mom, thank you for being such a wonderful mother, mother-in-law, grandmother, and great-grandmother. You are truly a "mother in Israel"! I am trying to be like you and follow in your steps (though I doubt anyone can, because you are so much like Jesus and follow Him so closely). You have been such a beautiful example of motherhood. On behalf of your natural family, your people in Portugal, and the family of God, we thank God for you. We love you!

Rachel Hattabaugh spent thirteen years in Argentina with her husband and three sons, who are all married now. Together her family raised up twenty-seven churches in Argentina before returning to California. Her son, Mark, who accompanied Sister Andrade to the Cape Verde Islands, is a pastor in Miami, Florida.

In 1994, only a few months short of her eightieth birthday, Sister Andrade made a brief visit to her beloved Portugal, where she was received with many tears of joy. Upon leaving she said, "The people I love are here, and I know God is continuing to care for them. It is enough; I am content. This time I leave in peace."

On July 20, 1996, at the age of eighty-one, Sister Andrade fulfilled her final mission. Still active, vibrant, and spreading her love and the love of the Lord everywhere she went, she died quickly while having dinner in a restaurant with Rachel. The doctor called it a heart attack. We call it divine intervention in a heart filled with love for Him, her family, Portugal, and all humanity.

Love is strong as death. . . . Many waters cannot quench love, neither can the floods drown it (Song of Solomon 8:6-7).

Sister Andrade in Portugal

*September 1988
in front of
church.*

*Elizabeth
Andrade in
Portuguese
costume.*

CHAPTER 19

Nancy Lassetter

COLOMBIA AND ECUADOR

Brother Lassetter and I grew up in Southern Baptist homes in Mississippi. As a child, I found strength in being at church as often as possible, even though my family was not particularly religious. We both had genuine repentance experiences.

While in college studying to become a social worker, I felt the drawing of the Lord to be involved after graduation in full-time Christian service of some sort. However, during that time in my life, Brother Lassetter and I met. I graduated from college and began work as a child welfare worker for the state of Mississippi. We married in 1965 and together began pursuing the goal of his preparation to become a college teacher. This took eleven years and occupied the first eight years of our married life.

After completing the Ph.D. in botany from Iowa State University, he accepted a teaching position at Eastern

Kentucky University. Upon moving there, we became active in a local Southern Baptist church. My husband was training to be a deacon, and we both were involved in Sunday school programs.

After a year, when we were thirty years of age we became very hungry for a deeper walk with the Lord. One night after a church service we talked about our dissatisfaction and the hunger in our hearts. Not knowing what to ask of the Lord, we prayed a simple prayer: "Lord, if there is anything else in the way of a religious experience that we can have, we want it. Please send it to us."

We knew nothing about the baptism of the Holy Ghost and had never known any Pentecostal people. There was no Oneness Pentecostal church in our city. However, Jesus is never limited by our circumstances, and when He heard the cry from our hearts, He put a plan into motion to bring to us the desires of our hearts. Little did we realize that night what wonderful things the Lord had in store for us!

Even though there was no Oneness Pentecostal church of any kind in our college town, God had been dealing with a family in another state for about two years about moving to our city to start a home missions United Pentecostal church. About a month from the time we prayed our simple prayer, they moved to our university town of about twenty thousand, and they moved into the vacant house right next door to us! They became our friends and taught us the *Search for Truth* Bible study. When God opened our eyes to His truth, we were baptized in Jesus' Name and received the wonderful gift of the Holy Ghost with the evidence of speaking in other tongues! We had asked the Lord for bread, and He did not give us a stone!

Being the first converts of a new home missions work was a special privilege, and with our pastor and his family we would visit neighboring churches for special services. In the first missionary service we attended, only a few months after receiving the Holy Ghost, we wept as if our hearts would break because of the missions need and the Spirit of God we felt. At that time we just assumed that all Holy Ghost–filled people responded in that same manner. This pattern continued in our lives. Each time we would hear a missionary, it would be like an emotional earthquake gripping us, and we would feel the results for weeks afterward.

We continued serving the Lord in the home missions church and received a lot of valuable training from our pastor and his wife. We accepted more responsibility in the church as time went on, and my husband continued advancing in his teaching position at the university.

The call of God on our lives to serve as missionaries came to each of us separately over a period of a year. A student named Luis Escobar from Colombia, South America, came to study at the university where my husband was teaching. He enrolled in one of my husband's classes and they became friends. As the year progressed, Brother Lassetter realized that the Lord was using Luis to call him to be a missionary, but he didn't tell me.

During this time, the Lord was also working in my life. The year before, I had a serious operation, and the Lord had done a lot spiritually in my life through that experience. I had come to the place of consecrating everything to Him, including our three daughters—Anne, Amy, and Carrie—material possessions, home, and security. Many times I was at the altar crying before the Lord and telling Him that everything I had was His to use in any way He desired.

At the end of that school year my husband still had not said anything to me about the call to the mission field. He knew that answering a call to missions service would totally change our lives. We would have to lay aside the professional career that we both had worked to attain, and our vocation would change. Leaving the United States behind, living in a foreign culture, and learning a new language would profoundly affect our whole family, especially our three daughters. Because of all this, my husband felt that I should also have my own personal call from God to missions service, so he asked God to put the same desire in my heart.

In May 1979, Brother Lassetter wanted to ask Luis to our home for a meal before he returned to Colombia. That was fine with me, because we had contact occasionally with students in his classes. Little did I know that Brother Lassetter had asked the Lord to do something special in my heart that night, if he had indeed received a definite call to missionary service.

The Lord did just that! Luis's visit will always remain a highlight of God's call in our lives. The presence of the Lord was manifested as we talked about Colombia that night. My husband and I wept with Luis as he talked of his love for his people. After the evening ended and Luis returned to his dormitory, my husband and I talked about all the Lord had been doing in our lives during the past year. We realized that God was calling us to be missionaries and specifically to Colombia, South America.

During the next few months, God confirmed our calling in many miraculous ways including a message in tongues with interpretation in a church where no one knew our circumstances.

The Lord dealt with us both in drawing us toward a country about which we knew very little. I was as excited about the challenge of the future as my husband was. Our call was to the ministry but included the missionary call from the very beginning. We were willing to do whatever would be necessary to fulfill our missionary call.

Our first contact, although unofficial, with the Foreign Missions Division was with Robert Rodenbush when he and Sister Rodenbush traveled through the Kentucky District during a Mothers Memorial drive. Later on, after making proper application, we waited on the timing of the Lord. The founding pastor of our church resigned, and we agreed to pastor the church until we received our missions appointment. Within a year, the Lord opened the door, and we were appointed in May 1981 as missionaries to Colombia. Our burden was to help establish a Bible school and be involved in training and teaching.

Immediately after our appointment, Brother Lassetter resigned his tenured professorship at the university and resigned as pastor of the church. We put our home on the real estate market, and we sold it to the first family that came to look at it. We bought a used motor home, sold our Volkswagen, and stored our belongings in Mississippi. Our family began a year of deputational travel with home schooling in our motor home when Anne was thirteen, Amy was nine, and Carrie was three years old.

After deputation, we spent a year in language school in Costa Rica, Central America, and arrived in Colombia in 1983. My husband helped establish and build the Bible school in the city of Cali. He taught classes, helped train Colombian teachers, preached, and taught special studies to pastors. I was also a teacher in the Bible school and taught some special studies to ladies and pastors' wives.

After two years in Colombia, escalating terrorism became extreme. Because of politics, the country was filled with anti-American sentiment. Kidnappings and street riots were common. The Lord let us find out that the Colombian who helped with housework during the day so that I could be involved in Bible school had been attending communist guerrilla meetings. We realized that our children were vulnerable as they rode the school bus two hours each day, that our house could be under surveillance, and that our telephone could be used for subversive purposes.

There were three missionary units at this time in Colombia. Because of the prevailing danger, the single lady missionary returned to the United States, resigning from missionary service, and the other missionary family returned for deputational travel. The Foreign Missions Division approved our request to move to Ecuador to complete the last year of our missionary term, and my husband traveled back and forth between Ecuador and Colombia during that year. He would cross the border into Colombia, travel in a small Piper Cub–sized airplane to Cali, and go straight to the Bible school in a taxi. He would stay inside, out of sight for two or three weeks at a time, and then return to Ecuador. I wouldn't know if my husband had reached Cali safely until he arrived back home in Ecuador, because he would not use the telephone in Colombia. The guerrillas had members in high positions and had connections everywhere, and Brother Lassetter thought they could be monitoring the telephone system.

Leaving Colombia was heartbreaking! It was more difficult for us to leave Colombia than it was to leave the United States to go to Colombia. Conditions did not improve but got worse, and we knew that with our young children we could not return. God had closed the door to Colombia, but our call to missions service was still vibrantly alive.

The future was uncertain, and we were apprehensive of the unknown. In prayer, the only light we could see in the dark tunnel of our life was Ecuador, where we had lived for a year. We followed this leading, trying to walk by faith and not by sight. We requested a transfer of field and were reappointed to Ecuador for our second term of service to work with three other missionary families. God had opened another door!

As we traveled on deputation in 1986-87, two of the families in Ecuador resigned from missionary service and left the field. A short time after we arrived in Ecuador the third missionary family also resigned and left. We were the only missionaries appointed to Ecuador! It was now evident that we had followed God's leading. Even when we were blind to God's plan and could not see or understand God's ways, He could see perfectly into our future.

Whereas in Colombia we felt a specific burden for Bible school work, God broadened our burden to other

areas as we worked in Ecuador. My husband was named
the field superintendent of Ecuador in 1987. During the
next nine years we would see the number of churches
grow to 287, with more than 250 additional preaching
points. Every church and preaching point was under the
direction of an Ecuadorian minister or helper. The number of licensed ministers increased to 131 and the con-
stituency to 14,000, both more than doubling, just like
the number of churches! In 1997, there were 4,500 in
attendance at the annual general conference, and 500
received the Holy Ghost there!

During our terms of service in Ecuador, our call has
remained as strong as it was in the beginning, and God
has let our ministry and burden grow to meet the needs
of the work. We have become increasingly involved in
administration, seminars, teaching, and leadership training. Ecuadorian teachers and administrators are now able
to operate the Bible school by themselves. Ecuadorian
pastors, ladies leaders, and youth leaders now have taken
the responsibility of a large part of the seminar training
and teaching, and write their own teaching material.
While we were in the United States for our most recent
furlough from 1996 to 1998, Ecuadorian leaders were in
charge of the work.

It has been a rewarding joy for me to work with the
ladies leaders and pastors' wives. They organize and
implement many activities and training seminars each
year. The ladies raise a yearly Dorcas in Action offering to
buy choice properties for church buildings. In a Third
World country like Ecuador with tremendous poverty,
when their annual offering equals several thousand U.S.
dollars it is easy to understand that they have captured
the vision of sacrificial giving!

If a missionary couple remains on the field a number
of years, many times the children who go with them in the
beginning will someday return to North America to live as
adults. For me, the ultimate reality of the missionary call

comes as we leave our precious children and grandchildren behind. Fear of the unknown, examining the call, letting go, uncertainty, and tearful good-byes are some of the emotions I experience as a mother and grandmother as we prepare for our fourth missionary term.

However, I have faith in my Savior, who has kept us through all our missionary experiences during the past sixteen years. The One who filled us with His Spirit and placed the call in our hearts many years ago is faithful, and He will keep us and our children close to Him! Anne, now thirty, is married to Art Townsley, and they have two children: Krista, ten, and Andrew, six. They attend the Full Gospel Church in Paw Paw, Michigan. Amy, now twenty-five, is married to David Bullens. They have one daughter, Brittany, who is four, and they attend Apostolic Tabernacle in Battle Creek, Michigan. Carrie, now twenty and a talented artist, is a junior at Mississippi College and attends First Pentecostal Church in Jackson, Mississippi.

Our call still affects our children and now includes our grandchildren, too. They all say good-bye to us as we leave to go to our country, and this is a sacrifice they give to the Lord because of our call. Next in importance to the pearl of great price, these treasures of my heart have been offered to Him as my most precious gifts that He might always keep them in His arms of protection and love!

Gift

by Carrie Lassetter

Lord, this means so much to me.
It's beautiful, precious,
Priced to be as costly as my life itself.
(At least in my mind, it's my wealth.)

My dream, my treasure—precious stone—
Lord, it's Yours, no longer my own.
It's my gift to You for eternity.
My treasure's now Yours—Yours only to see.

A virtuous woman is a crown to her husband (Proverbs 12:4).

Nancy Lassetter and the ladies leaders in Ecuador.

Nancy Lassetter teaching during the ladies service at the 1997 Ecuadorian national convention.

Brother and Sister Lassetter, Brother Daniel Scott, regional director of South America, and the Ecuadorian national board and their wives.

CHAPTER 20

Linda Poitras

NIGERIA AND GHANA

I was born in Tampa, Florida, to God-fearing parents who spent their lives trying to show me how to give myself totally to the Lord. My mother was the first Sunday school teacher I remember having, and my father was the only pastor I remember.

My family moved to Alabama in 1960, where my father built a new building and continued the church he had begun some twelve years previously in a little town called Opp. I remember the old church, but what I remember the most is working on the new building and having church in the city hall over the jailhouse while the building was being completed. I was seven years old when God filled me with His Spirit. My mother was right there with me, but my daddy was in his special room, travailing before God for the youngest of His children to be born into the kingdom. I was baptized in a little river near our town.

I was fortunate to grow up and spend my life in one town, because I didn't have the adjustments that many teenagers face today. God blessed our family, and my brothers and sisters all still serve the Lord today. I probably had as much uncertainty about serving God as any other teenager, and as graduation from high school drew near, I faced the same dilemma that others do—should I go to college, get a job, or go to Bible college? No matter how much I would have liked to attend Bible college, the money was just not there, and every door seemed closed. I finished two years at a junior college nearby and then moved onto the campus of the university I was to graduate from, which was made possible by scholarships. There was no church to attend, so I traveled back and forth every weekend to attend my home church, and I continued to be totally involved in the work of God with my family.

After graduation from college with a degree in music education, I began to look for a job. I finally found work in my hometown teaching private music lessons in the public school system. I can't say that I was totally satisfied to live with my parents, as all my classmates began to marry and have families, but it was good training for what God had in store for me later. I did find peace, fulfillment, and joy in working for Him at home, though, and I would not trade the extra years in my mother and father's home now for anything in this world!

At youth camp in 1977, the year I graduated from college, the Lord began to deal with me about what He wanted me to do with my life. During this time I almost made a mistake about a life partner. The Lord dealt with me about applying for the International Youth Corps that year, and I had already sent in my application before I became engaged. I'm so glad I listened to that still, small voice—it was certainly nothing earthshaking or drastic that caused me to break the engagement, just a certainty that God had spoken to my heart.

I traveled with the International Youth Corps to Alaska

that year in a life-changing experience. When I returned home, the Lord continued to deal with me about going somewhere, and my burden grew heavier and heavier. The Lord gave me some confirmation through men of God who knew me well, and my own family also confirmed that God was dealing with me about something special. I had no specific leading, except that I knew I was to go *somewhere.* I continued to work anywhere I could find to be used of God. And those were good years too, although I admit to being a little impatient while they were happening.

In his own time, God sent a missionary our way, and on an off-night service, God moved in our church in a way that no one there has ever forgotten. We had missionaries on a regular basis, but this was something unique! Johnny Garrison came to our church on a Tuesday night, and the church was packed to the brim. People were there that night whom we have never seen before or since. I don't know where they came from, but I believe God sent them.

The service was power packed from the beginning. I had been looking forward to meeting Brother Garrison, as he was related to one of the pastors in our section of the state. I had never heard of Nigeria and certainly had no premonition that God was going to tell me that night where I was going to go. I had never even thought of Africa as a possible place to work for Him, but He had been getting me ready for this for a long time. God visited us all that night in such a mighty way that our whole church, years later, is still talking about it!

When we were at home that night, sitting around the table after church, Brother Garrison looked across at me and said, "I believe somebody received a call to the mission field tonight."

I said, "Yes sir, and this is not the first time!" He was a little surprised, but he didn't know that God had been working on me for almost three years already! My family never questioned that I was to go to Nigeria—they all knew that God had spoken! Since I was the baby of the family, and an "old maid" (I was twenty-five years old), they all were a little protective of me, but God takes care of us even better than our families!

After Brother Garrison's visit, I began to inquire about the Associates in Missions (AIM) program. He helped me get approval from headquarters. He was supposed to return to Nigeria in May 1981. I was not able to finish my visa and passport work by then, so Brother Garrison called to tell me exactly what to do if I arrived in Nigeria and he was not able to meet me. And that is exactly what happened!

I traveled to Lagos as soon as I received my visa from Washington, and I had no way of contacting Brother Garrison as to the exact time of my arrival. I spent my first night in Nigeria in the international airport on a bench, with no way to communicate to the United States by phone or otherwise. I was completely cut off from all sources of help except the Lord, and I was scared. That was my first time to be so totally dependent on the Lord, and He didn't fail me!

I had to travel across town to the domestic airport the next morning, purchase a ticket, get my luggage all checked, get a boarding pass, and then take an hour's flight into the bush country. I arrived in Calabar, the capital city of the state where the Garrisons lived and worked, and still had a three-hour taxi ride into the bush before I reached the mission. I was too ignorant to be afraid and too close to my destination!

When I finally reached the mission compound and saw Brother Garrison, I was so relieved and happy that I couldn't do a thing but cry. God had brought me all the way to where He had called me! He always does!

I remained in Nigeria for three months that first time and then returned home on my twenty-sixth birthday to continue teaching school. I left knowing in my heart that I would be back; I just didn't know when. I spent two years at home, longing for news and contact with Nigeria the whole time. During this time, a young man from Canada was there, setting up the curriculum and administration of the newly constructed Bible school. He began to write to me, telling me of the people and places I so longed to know about. I was very pleased to receive all of his letters, but I never dreamed that there was any ulterior motive behind his writing. He returned to Canada in September 1983, and I went to Nigeria in October when Brother Garrison returned from general conference.

Meanwhile, this Canadian continued to write, and I answered his questions about the progress of the school. I continued to ask his advice about things he had begun there. And so, we became friends through the work of God. April 1984 was the scheduled time of the first annual youth convention in Nigeria, and Brother Garrison was pushing for this young man to return as a guest speaker. That suited me just fine, as I was anxious to turn all of these projects back over to the one who had started them in the first place!

Youth convention began on a Thursday night. Brother and Sister Garrison had to travel to Lagos to get a family from a nearby mission and collect this young man from Canada. That was fine, but they were supposed to return on Thursday in time for church. Well, they were delayed, and that left Candi Garrison, their teenage daughter, and me to make all the arrangements for sleeping, eating, and everything for the young people who had traveled to the headquarters for this special occasion. On top of that, I was sick all Thursday night and Friday.

By the time the Garrisons finally arrived, I was not in a very good mood! The Bible school students and youth department leaders did not know that Brother Poitras was our special guest speaker, so when he arrived that Friday afternoon they gave him an extremely warm welcome. I was so relieved that I didn't give him much of a welcome at all. He had been in close contact with my family, especially my mother, and was traveling with many personal things for me. But it took me a while to calm down enough to express myself properly.

Three days later, we had our first serious talk about working together and about the possibility that everyone was already talking about. Brother Poitras was concerned about my loneliness coloring our relationship, and he was also concerned for my family to accept and realize that this was the Lord's will before we proceeded very fast. Well, God always has the answers, and He didn't fail us again. God was in total agreement with our marriage, and He made all things possible in His own way.

The first year we were married was the toughest of my life. We returned to Nigeria after three weeks. We were in charge of ninety-three students at the Bible school (boarding students at that), one national staff member, twenty-seven churches, and the ministers involved in the district. We had only an AIM budget, of which we received only $12.79 for the first month we were back! On top of all that, various troubles caused the village to become restless enough to begin attacking the Bible school and students physically and also to threaten Brother Poitras's life continually. Those conditions were not the best for newlyweds, but again, God did not fail us. This was one of the many times that my own personal call was invaluable to our ministry, and there have been numerous others.

In September 1985, we returned to the United States to meet the Foreign Missions Board to apply for full appointment and were thrilled to be approved. Then we began our first deputational travel. God blessed us to finish in just thirteen months and return to the field after only fifteen months away. The Garrisons had been on location for most of six years and were completely worn out, so they returned to the United States in February after we arrived in January, with Brother Garrison nearly in a state of collapse. Again, our responsibilities were great, but God never failed us!

In February 1988, the villagers who had been tormenting us for several years got brave enough to mount an all-out attack on the Bible school, for which we were directly responsible. Brother Poitras was at the school that night when the town crier ran through the streets calling for everyone to join in the attack: "Kill the white man," and, to "Do it quickly!" My husband and an AIM worker managed to escape through the broken windows of the dormitory to call the police for help. Our students were scattered all over the area, and many of them were injured as they escaped through broken windows and ran for their lives. Several of our girls were attacked, but help arrived before they were molested. If I ever needed my own personal assurance that we were in the will of the Lord, it was then. God brought us through victoriously, and we could see His hand on us even then, but the trauma was intense.

All through my experiences in Nigeria, especially after I was married, it seemed as though when one of us was at our lowest as far as faith and assurance of God's plan for us were concerned, the other would be able to hang onto God's call. This fact kept us through "many dangers, toils, and snares" of the devil. It was not always easy for me to submit to the leading of the man whom God had chosen to guide my life, but it helped so much to know beyond any doubt that he was God's choice for me and also to know beyond any doubt that God had called both of us to work for Him there in Nigeria.

We were blessed with numerous AIM workers in Nigeria, which made it much easier to let go of the responsibilities that had occupied me for so very long. God always has an answer, if we will just wait for it!

The hardest thing I have ever done was to leave my mother and father and take my baby back to Nigeria, knowing full well some of the difficulties we would all face. Little did I know, however, that I would return to the United States to watch my father die of cancer and that he would never be able to play with or see my baby grow and learn. He never one time complained about this, though, and never rebuked me for taking her away from him. He had always taught me that the center of God's will was the only place to be happy, and he lived and died by that rule. My whole life's impression of him was dominated by his diligence and love of studying the Word of God. It was not easy to let him go, and it is not easy to think about leaving my mother now (she is in her seventies), but she has never tried to talk me out of going back, because she knows that God has called us to Nigeria. I praise God for parents like that.

I still marvel at the way God worked things out for me, and I have never regretted one minute of the time spent in Africa or felt I had made a mistake by heeding that still, small voice bidding me to go. I now look forward to the miracles that God is going to perform in my life, because without fail, when I put my trust in Him, He takes care of me and teaches me a little more about trusting Him again!

I conclude with the chorus of a song that God gave me before I went to Nigeria the first time. It is still so true of my life, and I can never praise God enough!

> *For my soul heard God's call,*
> *And I remembered His voice.*
> *It was a call for my heart and my life and my*
> *   time,*
> *And it gave me a choice.*
> *I could listen and heed or merrily go my own way,*
> *But I'm so glad I did choose*
> *My life for Jesus to use*
> *Each and every day!*

After eleven years of experience in Nigeria, West Africa, the Poitrases moved to Ghana, West Africa, to reopen the Bible school there and evangelize the country.

And when he putteth forth his own sheep, he goeth before them, and the sheep follow him: for they know his voice (John 10:4).

National Ladies President Linda Poitras speaking to Eastern Region ladies retreat in Ghana, West Africa.

Sister Poitras with special ladies in 1995. Left to right: Juliana Monie, regional ladies president; Gladys Coffie, regional ladies secretary of Greater Accra; Sister Poitras; Salome Anson, national ladies secretary; Else Lund, 26-year veteran missionary to Ghana.

Jim and Linda Poitras, eight-year-old Melinda, five-year-old Candra on Father's Day of 1997 in Accra, Ghana.

Sister Poitras working with musicians for the National Easter Convention, 1996, in Tema, Ghana.

CHAPTER 21

Margaret Carver

PAPUA NEW GUINEA, NEW ZEALAND, AND FIJI

I was born in Sydney, Australia, and was not brought up in a Christian home at all. I don't ever remember going to church—maybe just to Sunday school once or twice. But when I was a teenager, the Lord began to deal with me. I had a real desire to read the Word of God, so I asked my mother to buy me a Bible, which she did. I began to read and got really interested in the Scriptures.

About that time, I decided to go to a nearby Presbyterian church, and I also went to a dance there. It was a social activity for the young people, and they had invited neighboring churches. A young man came along from one of the other churches. I didn't know him at all, and we were not dancing together. In fact, I was dancing with someone else when he trod on my toe. He turned around and said to me, "Oh, I'm sorry."

At that moment, I looked at him and thought, Oh, he's

so handsome. I said, "Well, that's all right!" After that, I went to someone and asked who he was.

The girl whom I asked said, "His sister is in your class at school."

The next day at school I saw his sister and said, "I really like your brother; I met him last night at a dance."

She went home and told him that, and before I knew it, he had my telephone number. We began going out together, and together we began to study the Word of God. Even though we were just teenagers, we would read it, discuss it, and enjoy it.

When we read the Book of Acts, we began to see all these exciting things that we didn't see in the church where we were attending and began to question why we didn't see them. We went to the minister of the church and asked him about them. He said, "Well, things like healing and miracles and baptism are not important. They are not for the church today. They were for the early church, but you don't need to worry about them. They are not for you."

He was hoping perhaps just to get us to dismiss the subject, but we felt in our hearts that there was a church somewhere like the one we had read about. We read more and discovered baptism in Jesus' name. I don't know that we fully understood the importance of it, but we decided that it was important to be baptized. We even talked about baptizing each other. We thought perhaps we would go to a river. I would baptize my boyfriend. Then he would turn around and baptize me. We discussed doing that, but we decided that instead we would try some other churches. If the church we went to wasn't preaching what we felt it should, maybe there was another church that did.

We began to try all types of denominations, including most of the well-known denominations, independent groups, Roman Catholicism, and even a Jewish syna-gogue. A friend of ours who knew we were interested in different churches invited us along to a meeting. He said, "You have to come with me. This is a really different church." Little did we know that he was talking about Glen Bogue's church in Sydney. Brother Bogue was the pioneer United Pentecostal missionary to Australia. He came there in 1953, and we were searching for a church in 1967.

This young man had been just once to Brother Bogue's Pentecostal church in Belmore, Sydney. Since he invited us, we went along. He told us it was really different, and when we got there we believed him! It really *was* different. They were the noisiest group of people we had ever seen in church. They began by clapping and shouting and praising the Lord. We just didn't know what to make of it. We had never been in a church service like *that* before.

At the end of the meeting, someone came up to us and began to tell us how the Lord had healed their three-year-old daughter of spinal meningitis. That was really exciting to us. Here were people who believed in the same miracles as in the Book of Acts! It really got us interested, but we decided that we would just think about it.

It was a real shock to the system to be in our first Pentecostal service, so we began to try other churches. But in our hearts we felt that maybe this Pentecostal church really did have something. Over a period of six months, the Lord dealt with us and said, "Go back to that Pentecostal church." We decided we would go back; and when we returned six months later, we were baptized that very week in Jesus' name. I received the Holy Ghost, and about three months later my boyfriend received the Holy Ghost. That was how the Lord led us to this beautiful truth.

About a year after that, we were married by Brother Bogue. We stayed in his church for about a year, but then he returned to the United States. John Brian came as a missionary to Australia and became our pastor. My husband went to Bible school under Brother Brian, and for five years we stayed in the Belmore church working for the Lord.

While in Bible school, my husband saw a set of slides about Papua New Guinea. It stirred him, but he didn't tell me about it. It was a process of time before he actually told me his feelings about going there. But as the Lord continued to deal with him for a few months, he did tell me that the Lord had given him a burden for that country.

I was twenty-two, was a schoolteacher, and enjoyed my work. We had been married about two or three years and had just bought our first house. It was nothing special, but it was our first house. It was exciting as we redecorated and bought new furniture piece by piece. We had just bought a new set of furniture for the living room—a sofa and two reclining chairs—the first new set since we had been married. With the revealing of my husband's feelings for Papua New Guinea, I began to count the cost. Our house would be sold; our new furniture would have to go; our new baby would be parted from all family.

There was a real tug in my heart. Did I really want to hold on to these things, or did I really want what God had for our lives? That was really the first wrestling that took place in me. Those thoughts sobered me and made me realize that material things can certainly be a hindrance even when we don't want them to be. I wrestled with these things for weeks. I wanted to hold on to all these things, but at the same time my desire to serve the Lord was very real.

I loved the words of Jesus and read the Gospels often. His words in Luke 9:23-24 challenged me: "If any man will come after me, let him deny himself, and take up his cross daily, and follow me. For whosoever will save his life shall lose it: but whosoever will lose his life for my sake, the same shall save it." I decided that above all things I wanted to follow Him. Before long I was willing to sell everything, if that was what was necessary, and I would go. No one had taken this truth to that nation that lay north of Australia, one of the most primitive countries in the world.

We didn't have to meet a foreign missions board, because at that time the work in Australia was not organized to that point. We just met with Brother Brian, who was the missionary superintendent from the United States. He and Sister Brian were very encouraging about our going and so was the foreign missions director, who was a very elderly man. He had a real burden for missions. In fact, he made a visit to New Guinea before we did and tried to find a place that might be suitable for us. The Australian church approved of our going.

Our baby was three weeks old when we traveled to some of the churches, and a lot of people would make statements such as, "This has to be the most foolish thing you could think of to do, to take a baby to a country like that!" One young man was most irate and even abused my husband. It certainly was not very encouraging, but we felt that the Lord had definitely called us. He placed a confidence in my heart that it would be all right even to take a small baby into that place. Although I did not know a lot about the country where we were going, by this time I was excited and didn't have any fears.

As it happened, my father's job had just taken him over to England. He and my mother had gone across to England, so they had already left me. It was harder to leave my husband's mother, who had lost her husband about two years before. We were leaving her alone, and that part was especially hard for him.

The Lord never dealt with me personally about going to New Guinea, and I never had a particular burden for that country. I had never even thought about it in the sense of missionary work. When the Lord spoke to my husband, I didn't expect Him to have to speak to me about it, for I didn't feel that would be necessary at all. I had confidence (and still do) in my husband when he told me that he had heard from God. Therefore, I didn't feel that I had to have anything myself. I trusted in his call and wanted merely to be in partnership with this challenge.

I wasn't very concerned about having to learn a new language, because we would only need to learn a type of pidgin English, which was not a terribly difficult language and only took us about six months to learn.

We did have to sell our home and new furniture and leave them all behind. In 1973 with a six-week-old baby girl, we flew to Papua New Guinea. When we left Australia, the church there had no policy at all concerning a furlough, and we had no idea how long it would be before we could return to Australia. Nor was there a promise of payment each month. It was all an unknown adventure in trusting the Lord for everything.

For the first five years we lived in a very remote area of the country among primitive tribes of people. Our house was built of woven grass reed, with a tin roof in order to catch the rain for drinking water. The floor was woven bamboo, the refrigerator ran on kerosene, and for the first year we used kerosene lamps for lighting.

Our house was up in the mountains about six thousand feet. It was in a jungle, and the road was barely a road. The house was fifteen miles from the nearest small town, along a precipitous road hewn out of the sides of limestone mountains. The road was simply dug away by spade from the mountainside. In some places the workers had put stones along it to hold the tires on the road, and in other places they just left it as mud. Some of the sides of the mountain were one thousand feet down to the river, and the car had to travel along the very side of that mountain.

There were also fifteen bridges we had to cross. I used to count them as we went home each time, because most of the time those bridges were in very bad repair. The car would get to them, and there would be planks missing (taken for firewood), or they would be rotten. Always underneath there was a raging river. Then if it was wet, it would be slippery, and a car could easily slide off. Sometimes, the bridge was tilted at an angle. When a car went across, it could slip right off and down into the river. These crossings were the worst part and the most frightening experiences.

I can only imagine what the tremendous load of responsibility must have felt like to my husband to risk his family in such a way. He had to be very sure he was in the will of God and have a lot of faith that God could and would protect us. It certainly was not easy on him. Sometimes, Rachel, my little girl, would sense my anxiety and would begin to scream. We would both get out of the truck and walk across. But then my husband had to drive the truck, and it was just as distressing to watch the truck balance, slide, and crawl over the bridge.

These were difficult and lonely days for me. Occasionally I saw one other missionary lady who lived some miles down the valley from us. Many times I was reluctant to travel to town because it meant a return journey on that road.

There are many, many stories to relate concerning these early years. They were great years of leaning on and trusting in God. His Word became more precious, as it was all I had. I had to trust Him as a child would a father. I wouldn't exchange those valuable lessons!

Our son, Richard, was born while we lived in this situation. He was two months premature, and by the grace of God he was born in reasonable conditions for this country in a town about eighty miles away. I shall never forget traveling the treacherous, rough, and very bumpy road to the nearest town when I realized I was in labor. It seemed an eternity to get there and a miracle he wasn't born on the way! Richard weighed four pounds four ounces and was tube-fed for six days. When the tube was removed, I was told I could take him home.

I now had two small babies: Rachel was seventeen months when Richard was born. I once bought them a picture of two children crossing a bridge with an angel beside them. We hung the picture in their bedroom, and they always remembered that every time we crossed those bridges, there were angels holding us as we went across. These experiences have also definitely increased their faith and trust in God.

Sometimes on the field, I would feel that perhaps my children were not getting what everyone else had. I would remember people saying I was foolish to bring my baby to this country and sometimes wonder if they were right. However, looking back from these many years, I really wouldn't exchange the experiences for anything. I can say with all assurance that the Lord met every concern and situation with our children. The things I had thought necessary and that they really should have, were not necessary at all. They have not suffered for their many years in an underdeveloped country without friends and family of like country. Their situation is different from most because they were rarely in our own homeland of Australia. Nor were they at home in America. Neither Papua New Guinea, New Zealand, nor the Fiji Islands, where we now live, is really "home." Therefore, learning to adjust to the various cultures has not been easy for them, but they have both learned how to be flexible and to trust God in any situation.

It has not been to their detriment to change schools some nine times due to our changing circumstances; they have both excelled at school! Rachel graduated from high school, attended Kent Christian College in Dover, Delaware, and is now married to a fine, Christian young man. She has a desire to be a missionary, and she and her husband spent some time with us in Fiji on the AIM program. Our son, Richard, is with us in Fiji. He is the office manager of our headquarters, as well as a Bible school teacher, assistant pastor, and worker in the youth division. We are so grateful for our children's dedication to the work of God.

Concerning being a missionary, I have no regrets whatsoever. God has never failed us, nor will He ever. My family is very privileged to have been called to serve Him on the foreign field.

Let us hold fast the profession of our faith without wavering; (for he is faithful that promised) (Hebrews 10:23).

June Hughes

AFRICA

Hearing that his left arm would have to be amputated because of blood poisoning caused Roy Diehr to heed the admonition of his parents. They had faith that Roy would be healed if he would repent, be baptized, and receive the Holy Ghost. Not only did God heal Roy, but He also called him into the ministry. Shortly after that I was born, to his surprise, since the other two daughters were eight and seven years old. My parents named me, their youngest daughter, June.

From a very early age, I had a special love to follow Jesus. Because of the faith of my grandparents and parents, I also trusted God for healing as a child and cried to be baptized at the age of seven. While praying for the Holy Ghost, I said the words of the song, "I'll go where You want me to go, dear Lord, o'er mountain, or plain, or sea. I'll say what You want me to say, dear Lord; I'll be what You want me to be." God accepted that earnest prayer and filled me with the Holy Ghost. Through life this song has remained a reminder of my promise to God.

I attended large schools in Columbus, Ohio, but had no Pentecostal classmate. The home missions church my father pastored also lacked young people during my early years because of World War II. However, in 1945, the first youth camp was held at Buckeye Lake, Ohio, and that was the beginning of a new life for me. The anointed ministry of the Kinzie evangelistic party and the Nathaniel Urshans at the youth camps had a great influence on my dedication to God. Each year I rededicated my life to God and was willing to go, say, and be as God wanted. I made many lasting friendships during the three years I attended youth camp—and I eventually married one of those friends, John Paul Hughes, from Parkersburg, West Virginia.

After graduating from high school, I worked a year to earn money for tuition to Apostolic Bible Institute. Many times while I was in prayer at Bible college, God would bring to my mind the thought of being a missionary. One time, I was helping prepare the food for a class social. I didn't have much experience in a kitchen because my mother did all the cooking and the girls did the dishes. Not reading the directions correctly when preparing Kool-aid, I used hot water instead of cold, thinking it was like Jell-O. Even setting it outside in the snow didn't help much to cool it. Trying to encourage me, Sister Norris told me this was good training for being a preacher's wife. My reply was, "I'll never be a preacher's wife!" I wasn't remembering my prayer of dedication to be what God wanted me to be. Because of my mother's illness I only attended Bible college one and a half years.

Because John Paul attended another Bible college, we corresponded five years and were together at various holidays. John Paul was missions secretary of his class, his father was missions director at the church, and an older brother felt his call to be a missionary. Thus I realized, when I married John Paul that missions might be in our future. Since the church where my father pastored was very small, John Paul and I agreed to have our wedding in the tabernacle at the campground where we met. A large sign over the pulpit read, "Jesus Never Fails." Remembering that this sign was over us during our marriage ceremony has been an inspiration through the rough times.

At various times during our married life, God would ask me if I was still willing to go, and the answer was yes. But we were first to be put through a training course.

Being evangelists for the first nine years of our marriage gave us good training as far as being away from family, getting along with people, and living on a small budget. Evangelizing in North Carolina, where there were only two United Pentecostal churches, gave us a burden to start a church in that state. This was a lesson in faith, as we knew no one in the city, and we both would have to find jobs. During our twelve years of pastoring, I had a severe illness and was hospitalized. While in the hospital I had an experience in which it seemed that God was calling us to missions. However, the Lord had not spoken to John Paul.

The Lord knew that we needed Bible college teaching experience, so our next move was to Texas Bible College, where John Paul taught three years and I worked in the office. This was also where we developed a friendship with a pastor who later became a missionary. Close to the end of this missionary's term, he needed someone to help teach in the Bible school on his field so that the class could graduate before he left on furlough. The Foreign Missions Division asked us to stay a year while the missionary was home on furlough.

A few months before this missionary called from Africa for help, we had attended the general conference. The foreign missions service was always a highlight of the conference for us. This year, we were not sitting together during the missions service, and I was delighted when I saw John Paul go forward at the invitation to pray. In conversation after the service, he again indicated that he was willing to go but did not feel the call. By this time, the missionary burden was so great in my life that I went back to the motel room, crying and praying for God to please remove the burden if it was not His will for us to serve in missions.

There was a program that provided finances for short-term personnel. Since John Paul could find no reason to say no to the missionary's call for help, we left in May 1975 to Nigeria for what turned out to be the beginning of nineteen years of missionary service. During our eighteen months in Africa, we realized the need for someone to replace missionaries when they came home for furlough, especially where there was only one missionary in a country. We made application to be furlough replacement missionaries and were appointed to serve in Africa.

Serving in Kenya, we were required to learn Kiswahili, so we attended six months of language study. At our age, and as it was our first attempt to learn another language, the challenge was not easy. John Paul was good at cramming, but it took me hours of study and utmost willpower to finish the course. When John Paul made better grades on the tests than I did, my tears flowed because of frustration. With tears falling, I told the teacher I was determined to learn Kiswahili, no matter how long it took. With God's help, I did pass the course. Both of us found that when we started praying in Kiswahili, it became easier to speak the language in public. God overlooked our mistakes and knew what we were trying to say.

The Lord allowed us to remain in Kenya for three years, which was the first time in more than eight years that we had our own home, furniture, and dishes. Prior to this we used the house and furnishings of the missionaries we replaced. When the time came to sell, I had to do a lot of praying. I remembered my song of dedication to go, say, and be as God wanted. Then I started to sing, "I Surrender All," and victory came; singing it in Kiswahili made it sweeter. This experience again was preparing me for our next assignment.

Working in nine different African countries as missionary replacements prepared us for the position of regional field supervisor (now called regional director) for Africa, which began in 1988. We spend the majority of our time traveling among our beloved missionaries on that continent and thank God for His hand on our lives.

Brother and Sister Hughes recently retired for a short time and bought a home. After twenty years, she is able to have her own home part time. In January 1997 the Hugheses became teachers in the international teaching ministry.

For here have we no continuing city, but we seek one to come (Hebrews 13:14).

Sister June Hughes is teaching a ladies seminar in western Kenya under the trees. Brother Moses is interpreting, and Darline Kantola Royer was also a teacher.

Brother and Sister Hughes with a Malagsy Bible school couple that was sponsored through the ladies Bible school fund.

Sister Erknesh, Nona Freeman, and June Hughes in Sister Erknesh's home with the "welcome cake" given by one of the pastors.

Diola Willoughby

SPAIN

The Lord first spoke to me about missions when I was eight or nine years old. Brother and Sister Ellis Scism were showing slides of India when the Lord spoke to my heart, "Someday you will see this in person." I almost forgot about this experience as I grew up, thinking that I wanted to be an airline stewardess or a legal secretary.

In my first year out of high school I traveled around the world with Brother and Sister Carl Adams and their daughter, Sandra. We visited nineteen countries in six months. Our main visit was to India, where we stayed for three months. My childhood experience came back to me, and a new burden began to flame in my heart. When I saw the great need throughout the world to teach people the wonderful plan of salvation that God had prepared for them, I wanted to dedicate my life to missions. At the time, I assumed it would be India where I would fulfill my calling, but the Lord had other plans.

After I returned to the United States, I enrolled in Conquerors Bible College to prepare myself. There I met a young man named Bill Willoughby. He told me about an experience when he was fifteen years old that gave him a burden for Barcelona, Spain. He felt that someday he would go to Barcelona, but "probably as a teacher."

Throughout Bible college, Bill felt called more as a teacher than a minister or pastor. As our relationship became more and more serious, this bothered me. I wanted to marry a minister who wanted to become a missionary. That it might be Spain, not India, didn't bother me, because India appeared to be closing its doors to resident missionaries. I had also taken some Spanish, which would definitely help.

Several of my friends advised me against marrying him, because they didn't think I'd be able to fulfill my missionary calling if I were married to him. I prayed for God's guidance and wisdom, and at last I decided that there was no one else I'd be as happy with as William Ellis Willoughby III. I decided to leave his calling in the hands of the Lord.

Too often, a wife tries to push her calling onto her husband. Or she tries to give him a calling herself, instead of allowing God to do the work. May God help the couple who goes to the mission field on the wife's calling!

It is hard to wait patiently for God's time. For us, it was ten years after we were married. Four couples who were our friends at Bible college were appointed ahead of us. Sometimes I wondered if we would ever be on the mission field.

Shortly after we were married, my husband received his local license. This greatly encouraged my dream. Then, he did his ministerial internship in Philadelphia. This Idaho farm girl considered herself on her first mission field! The Lord was just preparing me for life in the big city of Barcelona with its four million lost souls.

After finishing our time in Philadelphia, we went to be the assistant pastor to a small work in Oregon. Within a few months, my husband ended up being the pastor. Seeing the growth of the work in Oregon gave us a lot of foundational experience. The work in Barcelona would have to begin from scratch.

Next, Bill talked with the Foreign Missions Board. They advised him to finish his education before applying for the field, saying it was becoming increasingly necessary to have a certain occupation in order to obtain visas in many countries.

Much to my disappointment, we went to college instead of to the mission field. By this time, our daughter, Kristina, was born. However, I was still able to get a year's work done toward my degree.

After his graduation, Bill became the principal-supervisor of an Accelerated Christian Education (ACE) school. I taught kindergarten and first grade. I kept asking the Lord, "What has this got to do with being a missionary? Will we never be able to go?" Later, I used this greatly valued experience as I taught my children at home, due to the high cost of private education. In our last year in Spain it was also necessary for me to be the supervisor of the ACE mission school where our children attended with twenty others from various missions.

During the summer of 1977, in a time of prayer, the Lord quickened to my heart in a vision that the time was near for us to go to Spain. Three weeks later, Bill was hired to teach at Gateway College of Evangelism. I consoled myself that at least it was closer to headquarters in St. Louis and the Foreign Missions Board.

While there, I was able to finish my degree. My instructors will never forget me. I entered college on crutches with a broken leg, and our son, William Ellis Willoughby IV, was born in the middle of my student teaching. When he was a month old, we were finally appointed as missionaries. My dream came true! I finished my algebra by correspondence. In spite of the difficulties involved, the mission board allowed me to leave the deputational trail long enough to go receive my B.A. in elementary education.

It was a surprise to everyone—especially us—that we were actually appointed the first time. Our friends at headquarters had said, "They almost never appoint first-timers." The first thing the regional field supervisor said during our interview was, "I want you to know that I'm not recommending that anyone be appointed to Spain right now." Our shrimp dinner didn't want to go down and kept trying to swim back up. At the end of the interview, he was impressed enough to say, "Well, maybe I'll change my mind. I'll keep praying about it."

The next day we faced the Foreign Missions Board. This was the worst part for me; I certainly dreaded it the most. My insides felt as if they had been through a blender. Once we were inside, however, and I saw all their kind faces and smiles, I began to relax. The questions they asked weren't hard; they just wanted to feel our burden. The most beautiful part was when they gathered and prayed for us and the glorious presence of the Lord filled the room.

The news of our appointment was hardest on the grandmas, for they wouldn't get to see their grandbabies grow up. One said, "They didn't ask to be taken to such a faraway, strange country. Is it fair to them?" My biggest fear was the condition of the medical facilities. "God, I guess I am going to have to rely on You more completely!" I finally decided.

After finally being appointed and announcing the news to friends and relatives, the real test came: deputational travel! We began traveling in a motor home when Wil was four months old. He got his first tooth in Missouri, learned to crawl in Nebraska, learned to walk in Louisiana, and had his first birthday in Michigan. I taught Kristina first grade through a correspondence course.

She did fine but never did get a good grade in handwriting. I wonder if that was because of the bumps on all those roads.

Despite the wild and horrid tales about the deputational trail, after three times of trudging for thousands of miles around the United States, we can number our distasteful experiences on one hand. In retrospect, they weren't really that terrible either. Once we kept seeing a big cockroach swim back to the top of the banana pudding each time the pastor's wife dipped out a big scoop. My husband has never eaten banana pudding since, but my bowl tasted fine. Another time we were asked to go to an unscheduled service. A big offering was taken after it was announced that it would go to us. But we didn't receive any offering.

A couple of times we didn't receive any fellowship from the pastor or his family. A few times I wasn't even sure who the pastor's wife was. Once we came to hold a missionary service and then found out it was actually a three-day rally. Brother Willoughby was only allowed a couple of minutes to say a few words, and we were mostly ignored the rest of the time. Once when Brother Willoughby was traveling alone, he was let into the church by the church secretary a few minutes before the service started. He preached his heart out and prayed a man through to the Holy Ghost. The secretary showed him out, locked the door, and left. He received no offering, food, or motel arrangements. He did finally find a motel but ended up sleeping in the car since the room was crawling with roaches.

Nevertheless, there were hundreds of other churches that treated us like royalty. They planned special things for the children, took up special offerings for them as well as for us, put us in evangelists' quarters or in a hotel so we could have a break from the motor home, and so on. It seemed that after every bad experience, God would send us to a church that more than doubly blessed us.

I tried to remember that a pastor's wife is human, too. Some were so shy, especially young ones, so I'd try to make the first effort to put them at ease and treat them as I wanted to be treated. One area that could cause misunderstandings was not having the time of arrival and dinner and sleeping arrangements clearly understood by both parties. In order to avoid problems and inconveniences to our hosts, we tried hard to stick to the agreement or call if something caused an unavoidable delay.

As the time of departure drew closer, we began to believe that we were actually going, and our hearts started pounding faster. As we sold all the things that we decided wouldn't fit into our two four-by-four-by-eight-foot wooden crates or the eight K-Mart footlockers, a wave of advance homesickness hit me. We sold Kristina's new birthday bike, Wil's baby bed and high chair, my high school graduation gift sewing machine (Bill had bought me a new one), the rocking chair we bought the day Kristina was born, the old washer and dryer (thank God for Ladies Auxiliary, who replaced them), and we gave away the piano I had had since I was eight years old. Each time something left, an invisible blow chipped another small piece of my life and my heart away.

One of our last services was in a camp meeting with several thousands of people. Suddenly the thought gripped me: It's going to be an awfully long time before I ever feel or see something like this again. I tried to memorize the sight of all the uplifted hands and the sound of the singing and praying.

During the moments of departure, I wondered, Will all of these loved ones be here when or if we come back? I tried to impress the sound of their voices, their features, and the feel of their embraces deeply in my heart to help me recall them in my lonely hours ahead. Many times it wasn't easy or even possible to hold back the tears.

Three weeks later, however, we stood high up on the Mt. Juich Fort walls, gazing at the sparkling Mediterranean waters in the Barcelona port that crowds four and a half million souls in a valley with a ten-mile radius. They are housed in towering *rascacielos* (skyscrapers) of the twenty-first century as well as palatial homes of ancient times. Then a great joy sprang up within, and I could truly say, "It was worth it all!"

Sister Willoughby happily followed her husband to Spain and stood by him in the work until he felt it time to return ten years later. They are currently pastoring Greater Faith Tabernacle, a United Pentecostal Church in Nacogdoches, Texas.

Blessed are ye that sow beside all waters (Isaiah 32:20).

We prayed all night, and she received the Holy Ghost by singing in tongues about 4:00 A.M.

Arriving home from youth congress in Manheim, Germany, in August 1988.

Our first Sunday School Christmas program.

Praying with Charo, who later received the Holy Ghost and was baptized in the precious name of Jesus in the Mediterranean Sea.

Bible study with Juanita and her family. She later was baptized and filled with the Holy Ghost in spring of 1989.

CHAPTER 24

Linda Walmer

BRAZIL

I am glad that we don't have to be of any certain family, race, wealth, or area of the country for God to speak to us. If we had to belong to a special category, then there would never have been a place for me. No one ever heard of my family, for they were not in church.

My parents divorced when I was twelve. I possibly blocked out my feelings because I can scarcely remember it concerning me much either then or now.

When I was twelve, a girlfriend, Joan Gleason, invited me to her Sunday school. Her father had just moved his family to Albany, Oregon, where they rented a dance hall to hold services in. I went with her and loved it! As I recall, only nineteen people were present, yet I felt so good to be in that place with its friendly, loving spirit. I couldn't wait to go back to the next service.

Although the church was small, we always felt God's

sweet presence. I would cry at the altar and go home with my eyes swollen. Mother would ask me, "What is wrong at that church that you always cry?" I would try to explain about how God blessed the people, but Mother could never understand why that would make anyone cry. She never forbade me to go, however, so I never missed a service. The Lord filled me with His Holy Spirit and began speaking to me about serving Him in a greater manner.

As a teenager I remained tender to the things of God. Because I had such a longing to please the Lord, the things of the world never held a great attraction for me. Missionaries would visit our church, and I would be on the front row taking in every word.

God led me to Conquerors Bible College in Portland, Oregon, where I met a fine young man, Phillip Walmer. We married in 1961 and graduated from Bible college in 1962. We wanted to work for God and were willing to go anywhere and do anything. We just didn't know for sure where or what He wanted.

We assisted a pastor in Oregon City, Oregon, for about a year. A son was born there. We then moved to Washington to open a work in Bellingham. Our second son was born there. We had our first service when he was two weeks old and our other son was fourteen months old. Somehow, we bought a building, stayed five years, and saw people saved. We then moved to a place where the work was about five years old, and we labored there for five years.

As the years passed and two more children were born, we experienced many of the ups and downs of life. Yet always, the desire to serve God was preeminent. Could it be that we would go to the mission field? Who, us? We had no special talents and no fame. We were only a couple who wanted to win souls for the Lord.

As we pastored two churches, we scheduled many missionaries to minister to our congregations. Each time a family would come by, we felt, Is the Lord calling us?

Does the Lord want us to go? Where? No real answer came.

In 1970, we attended the general conference in Portland, Oregon. During the foreign missions service Brazil was mentioned as having many cities of millions of people with no missionary or even a national worker. Actually very little was said, but a great need was presented, and we were deeply touched. We knew Brazil was the place we would go.

We were afraid to tell anyone, so we didn't speak of it to others until the Bennie DeMerchant family came by our church about two months after conference. Before we could serve them dinner, we couldn't contain it a moment longer, and so we spilled the news to them. They encouraged us to come and gave us some ideas of what to expect when we got there. We began to study the Portuguese language, which is spoken in Brazil. We read books, wrote letters, called the missionaries, and prayed, prayed, and prayed some more.

In 1971, we applied to the Foreign Missions Board for appointment to Brazil. It was an indescribable blow to us when the answer came back, "Wait." We thought our world had come to an end. Brazil needed us. Couldn't the board see that?

We had told our church that we were applying, because of our great confidence that we would be appointed. It was extremely difficult to return in our saddened condition, but we firmly intended to apply again the next year.

God never stops leading if we allow Him. We continued to pray, to study Portuguese, to read books about Brazil, and to write letters to the missionary families: the DeMerchants, Bakers, and Norrises.

In 1972, we applied again. This time we were appointed! We were excited, but at the same time I had certain fears about taking my four children to this new country. Would it be safe? What kind of house, or hut, would we have? What about the children's education, and so on?

We started deputational travel, and we traveled for about a year. Although we had applied early for permission from the Brazilian government to enter Brazil, the visa still had not come by the time we finished. We had to wait another nine months for it to come. In the meantime, we lived in our motor home by a church until we were finally able to sell it. The nine months seemed more like nine years as we endured the daily frustration of waiting for the mail to bring that notice. Finally, the waiting was over. The notice came, and within thirty days we were in Brazil.

In spite of having to meet the board twice, the long wait after deputational travel, and the many trials and difficulties on the field, we have never once doubted our call. Having problems does not mean someone is out of the will of God. All of us have problems, wherever we live.

All of our children have always loved Brazil. Today our son, Michael, his lovely wife, Yvonne, from Uruguay, and their little boy are fully appointed missionaries to Brazil, and we are very thankful for that.

After over twenty years in missionary service and the many things that have happened, God still renews the call in our hearts. It has meant saying good-bye to those we love, knowing all will suffer the loneliness of the separation. Only prayer can keep the call strong and alive.

Thank God for His wonderful love that has kept me close to Him!

It's an old saying but true nonetheless: "Only one life that will soon be passed; only what's done for Jesus will last."

Which hope we have as an anchor of the soul, both sure and stedfast (Hebrews 6:19).

CHAPTER 25

Judy Addington

NEW ZEALAND

Into each of our lives will come experiences that cause us to question the purpose. One such incident occurred in our lives that perhaps will, in some measure, encourage others to look beyond the here and now to beyond—beyond our limited understanding—and find strength for today and hope for tomorrow.

One bright and sunny November morning a little girl, our sunshine, burst upon our world. My husband and I were so happy to have a healthy, bouncing baby girl: Jananna Marie Addington. She was a big little girl (nine pounds five ounces), and due to complications of a cesarean section, our hospital stay was longer than usual.

One day in my hospital room with Jananna, I gave her the complete inspection—checking her fingers, toes, and so on—and proceeded to have a personal dedication of my sweet little girl between my Lord and me. Recently, friends of ours had been in the throes of heartache because their children who had been reared as Christians had now in their later teens turned their back on God. What grief those parents felt! What turmoil faced the youngsters! I didn't want that for us or our little daughter. I prayed specifically that she would be used for God's glory, that she would serve God all her life, and that her life would be instrumental in bringing souls into His kingdom. It was a special time between Jesus, Jananna, and me.

Time went on. We had our first daughter dedicated as we do in our Pentecostal churches. At the time my husband and I were assisting in our local church and were very active in its functions. As we proceeded with the ups and downs of life as usual, Jananna turned one year old. Soon the holiday season was upon us. But this year I felt a heaviness overshadowing all of the festive activities. Although I had very real concerns for the health of my father at the time, I put my uneasiness down to the strain of having the flu during this busy season.

The fourth of January was a bitterly cold Sunday, and because I was sick with the flu, I didn't attend either the Sunday morning or evening service—something very unusual for me. I loved church and working with people. I directed youth choir on Sunday mornings and had five Sunday school teachers under me in the Junior Class. On Sunday nights, I directed the adult choir.

Then tragedy struck. On Monday morning, January 5, our little daughter was dead. An autopsy determined that death was caused by SIDS (sudden infant death syndrome). Our world was turned upside down.

The devil doesn't show sympathy when we are down. He inspired a woman to tell us as we left the funeral home that we should never have other children and prophesied that the same thing would happen to them if we did. But the devil is the father of lies; such words hurt, but we trust in Jesus.

Jananna was buried on Thursday, January 8—on her

fourteen-month birthday. On Friday we attended an all-night prayer meeting, and while there I asked the Lord the ultimate question anyone in my position would: "Why?"

Immediately in my heart I heard His question, "Do you remember when you dedicated Jananna to Me?" My mind zoomed into that hospital room fourteen months ago when I dedicated her to Jesus. "Did you mean what you said?"

"Oh yes, Lord!" I reviewed my commitment and started to look for something good in what to me was something so awful.

At the time, my husband and I were the managers of 180 apartments. Many had come to offer their condolences, and I looked for any opportunity to direct these people to Jesus through our time of sorrow. The funeral director and his mother also spoke many times of the difference they observed in us—how we reacted to this grief. As a result they came to church, and she received the Holy Ghost. Tenants of our buildings started visiting church, and before we transferred to another state two years later, at least six had come to know the Lord. How many since then I do not know. And through it all I did find some sense of consolation, knowing Janie had in some small way come to help those in our world find Jesus to be real in their lives.

Time went on. We assisted in another church and then took the pastorate in the city of Anamosa, Iowa. Life was good; God blessed our feeble efforts as we sought more of Jesus.

Then in 1984 a dream came true. We had always had a burden for missions, but when God opened the door for us to become missionaries to New Zealand, it was a new step in our walk with God. A dream became reality! We were actually going to another country to share what Jesus had done for us and what He would do for those far across the world.

With such an awesome task on the horizon, we spent

much time in prayer. One day while praying, I thought of our children and how this move would affect them. What would happen in their future? By now we were blessed with a beautiful little girl, Janell Bethany, and a wonderful son, Matthew Wayne. I had also placed their future in God's hands. But even so, as with all mothers who have buried children, my mind went back to my Janie. "O Lord, just think if Janie would have been here, how many more people she could have been instrumental in winning for You Lord, how many more souls for Your kingdom."

And then a sweet assurance seemed to sweep over me when a still, small voice said, "But Jananna is still winning souls, and she will continue to win souls in New Zealand, for every soul that comes to know Me through you will have been seeds planted by Jananna." The more I thought about it the more I began to understand. Yes, Janie's life and death changed our lives and my husband's ministry in so many ways. We now had a compassion that we would never have had. We could understand the pain and tragedy of others, and yet we knew the God of comfort, the God who cannot fail, who is so close to the broken-hearted. We could share His compassion with conviction.

Our missionary service in New Zealand has been a growing and learning experience with many wonderful memories. Many lives have been touched and changed by touching Jesus, and yet there have been many heartaches and disappointments. Still, the burden remains to help others find the heart mender. Through it all, I thank God for the life experiences and for the brothers and sisters in the family of God who have prayed, supported, written, and given. We are so blessed!

We await His call to "come up higher" when we shall see Him face to face and bask in the love of those who have gone before. Until then, I do not know what tomorrow holds, but I know who holds my hand. His hand is ever extended, reaching out for the oppressed. Even when things in life seem purposeless, God can take the most horrible circumstances and work good from them. Each of us needs to place our hurting, bruised, and broken pieces into the hand of the heart mender and let Him make us whole, for to everything there is a purpose.

To every thing there is a season, and a time to every purpose under the heaven (Ecclesiastes 3:1).

Bob and Judy Addington at the School of Missions, 1996.

Richard and Margaret Carver and Bob and Judy Addington, New Zealand.

Judy Addington reading poem over the grave of daughter, Jananna Marie.

Bob and Judy Addington with Jonathan Downs at the South Pacific Regional Conference, 1996.

CHAPTER 26

Abigail O'Keefe

SIERRA LEONE

I was born into a Catholic family in Maui, Hawaii, and remained a Catholic until I was about fourteen years old. My family was converted by some close friends who were Pentecostal.

When I was a little older, I attended the Apostolic Bible College in Tulsa, Oklahoma, and even evangelized a little before I got married. I had never really intended to marry a minister, but I did. We assisted in a church in Pittsburgh and then started a home missions church in Antioch, California. We pastored there for eight years. During this time, my husband served the Western District as its foreign missions director. While in Antioch, we had a nice building, I had a lovely home, and we dearly loved the people who came to the Lord through our church.

My husband never mentioned to me that he would someday be a missionary until after we were married.

Then I learned that he had always had in mind that one day he would go to the foreign field, but I still had no idea where. In fact, I put it out of my mind and enjoyed all the good things of my present situation.

When he came to me to pray one day and said we would be going to Africa, I was completely stunned. I was upset about it, but I did not oppose any of the necessary preparations involved with the Foreign Missions Division in St. Louis. I still wasn't ready to say yes, however.

My husband asked me to pray about it, but I was so discouraged and downhearted that I just *couldn't* pray. Finally, one day I decided that I had to pray and ask the Lord to help me, because I just couldn't do it without His help. I wept and asked the Lord to give me assurance that He would take care of my family and our three boys. It seemed as if the Lord sat next to me in that room and told me He would take care of us, and that I should not stand against my husband. To that, I could say nothing, nor ask any questions.

We didn't tell anyone that we were going to apply for missions work. Thank goodness we hadn't, for we were turned down! This way, no one knew and didn't get upset or disappointed; we also didn't have to answer a million questions from friends and family. We were very disappointed, however. There are just no words to describe that crushing feeling of being denied to do what you feel so strongly that God wants you to do.

Nevertheless, I knew that we would apply again, and I was all for it. We felt that we should trust the board to be on our side. We prayed for them to send us when conditions were right and when they felt God was ready for us to go. That was extremely hard to understand at the time! In spite of our tremendous disappointment, it did not stop us and we did apply the next year. We were accepted. By then, I was more than glad to sell my home and was excited about the whole thing. Our families did not interfere, for they knew that one day we would be on the field; however, it still broke our hearts to leave them.

The only fear I had was for the boys. I did not want them to get discouraged serving the Lord, among other reasons. Remembering my prayer, I trusted Him to take care of them.

We have now been missionaries for over twenty years, having gone on the field in 1975. The Lord has really blessed our family. We have been in good health, and my boys studied at home through correspondence school without any major problems. The Lord told me that He would take care of us, and He has. Of course, now my boys are back in the United States, and Brother O'Keefe and I are here with just our little pet poodle.

We were the first UPC missionaries in Sierra Leone. The Lord has blessed us in the work there, and I can honestly say that I have no regrets about coming to the field—even to Africa, which I so dreaded and feared in the beginning. We have seen many wonderful results and seen the Lord move in mighty ways. Trusting the Lord enough to follow my husband anywhere, has been the best thing I have ever done. I can't praise the Lord enough for allowing me to go.

In the book *Mountain of the Lion* read the story of the great revival in Sierra Leone, West Africa, and the battles fought to give birth to and sustain the revival.

And they called Rebekah, and said unto her, Wilt thou go with this man? And she said, I will go (Genesis 24:58).

Brother and Sister Donald O'Keefe.

Abigail O'Keefe with winnow in village, Sierra Leone.

Abigail O'Keefe cooking in village, Sierra Leone.

CHAPTER 27

Susan Tracy

PAKISTAN

I was born in Fort Fairfield, Maine. At that time my mother was a backslidden Pentecostal, but my Dad had never been acquainted with Pentecostalism. It wasn't until I was two years old that my mother gave her heart to God. My dad took the news of her conversion well. After staying up all night thinking about this change in their lives—no drinking, smoking, parties, and so on—he told my mother that he would never try to stop her or the kids from going to church and serving the Lord.

Our family moved to Massachusetts when I was five years old. We attended the United Pentecostal Church in Foxboro, Massachusetts, pastored by George Cook. I received the Holy Ghost during the annual summer camp meeting in Pea Cove, Maine. Winfred Black from St. Louis, Missouri, was our camp speaker. He took all of those attending who had not yet received the Holy Ghost into the prayer room, where he talked to us of the greatness of God and how we could yield ourselves to Him completely, thereby receiving His Spirit. I was eight years old at the time. My expression on being asked how I felt receiving the Holy Ghost was, "I feel like a coffee percolator . . . all bubbly inside!" His joy is still my strength! Upon my return home to Massachusetts, my pastor baptized me in Jesus' name.

My husband and I met when we were young, before we were out of high school. He lived in New Brunswick, Canada. His training was in electrical design drafting. When we married on July 22, 1967, he was doing electrical drafting for an engineering firm in Hamilton, Ontario, Canada. He was active even during this time as youth leader, Sunday school teacher, and eventually Sunday school superintendent. He received his bachelor's and master's degrees through an external program of Indiana Bible College.

Upon yielding ourselves more and more to the will of God and through the following of His leading, we left Hamilton, Ontario, to help another young couple open a work in St. Catharine's, Ontario. By this time, we had one child, a son. During this time in the United Pentecostal Church, the Home Missions Division called this type of work "tent making," because the apostle Paul worked as a tent maker while helping the work of the gospel.

We left St. Catharine's with two children and moved to New Brunswick, where my husband worked as an Electrolux vacuum cleaner salesman for a while and worked in the church as the youth leader and a teacher. He eventually got a job with the Irving Pulp Mill, and we built our second home.

We did all we could to help the local pastor, and we traveled on some weekends to help vacationing pastors in their churches. We continued to feel a call to greater service for the Lord. During one of our weekends away, we ministered in song and the Word to the church in Hatfield

Point, New Brunswick. A few days later, the pastor called to tell us that the church had voted us in as their assistant pastor. Surprise! Would we come?

After praying about it, we felt an assurance that this was where God was leading us, and we agreed to come. We moved to Hatfield Point, and during the next year, on my husband's thirtieth birthday, we were finally in full-time ministry.

We helped with their new building program, since the old church was full and expansion was needed. We were so excited to be finally working in a closer way for God! Neither time nor paper permits me to relate all the experiences we encountered there, but it was a time of learning and growing for us.

In the spring of 1978, my husband went with two other men to five countries in South America. He was trying to find the will of God for his future involvement. We had both been feeling the move of God towards giving more of ourselves and took this opportunity to check on overseas ministries. After being away three weeks, he returned a changed person. He had no definite call for South America, but he knew the calling was somewhere overseas. After the pastor resigned, we became pastor and stayed approximately two years.

While pastoring in Hatfield Point, we had a visit from Donald Hanscom, missionary to Pakistan. Because the Lord had been dealing with both my husband and me about a change in our lives, we were open, listening and questioning Brother Hanscom constantly during his two-day visit. The way we bombarded him with questions, he must have felt that he was being given the fifth degree! The minute he left our home, we both fell into each other's arms, realizing immediately, as if God had audibly spoken, that, without a shadow of a doubt, God was leading us in a missionary direction.

We filled out our preliminary application in December. Then a formal application had to be completed, followed by a visit to our home from Paul Cook, the regional field supervisor for Asia. At the 1978 general conference in Kansas City, Missouri, we met the Foreign Missions Board.

When we went to Kansas City for our interview, our feelings were in a turmoil. We prayed that the Foreign Missions Board would have the mind of God for our lives in their decision. Whatever the decision, we had made up our minds that we would accept it as God's will for our lives at that time. We did receive our appointment on our first interview, which was then followed by a ratification by the General Board.

I can honestly say that the material things in my home had no hold on me. Once God confirmed what we were feeling, we never looked back. We had our final service at the church in Hatfield Point on New Year's Eve, December 1978. Both of our families accepted this as God's will for us, even though they were saddened at losing us for four years until we would return again for deputational travel.

Our first deputational travel was one of the shortest on record. We began and ended in nine weeks, arriving in Pakistan on April 18, 1979. The first two weeks were quite an experience. The country of Pakistan was dirty, smelly, and hot upon our arrival. (We had to leave the United States bundled up for winter.) For the first two weeks we stayed with Brother and Sister Corcoran in Lahore.

I cried every night for almost two weeks. I began to realize the differences from being in a Christian country and the closed-in feeling of a Muslim society. Talk about culture shock!

We worked on getting entrance into the Missionary Language School in Murree Hills. After two weeks, we went and spent the summer months there studying the Urdu language for six hours a day, with tutoring and private study afterwards. My husband returned to Lahore to oversee the construction of the Lahore Bible School in the absence of Everett Corcoran, who went on furlough.

Our children went to the Lahore American School for two years. Then we moved to open a new work in the capital city of Islamabad. Because of the extremely high cost of schooling in the capital, we decided to teach our children at home through the ACE program. I set up one room as a schoolroom and began each school day at 9:00 A.M. on the dot! I was our children's teacher for three hours a day. God had to help us all!

Yes, there were times of discouragement. My dad, in our first year in Pakistan, was diagnosed with cancer of the throat. He battled this disease until 1988, with eight operations. There were times that I wanted to go home, but there was no money for such a trip. Discouragement with the language and culture barriers, worry about health problems in a country with squalid conditions, and so on, made us pray more fervently that God's hand of protection would cover us. The adjustments to a new way of life were less for the children, for they were small: ages nine, six, and five. Adjustments at their ages were much easier because their parents were with them—this was their security.

We returned for our second furlough in 1987. We were unable to get our visas for returning to Pakistan, but God had something else in mind. While we were again asking God for new direction for our lives, He was still working. We were approached by the Foreign Missions Division for the position of regional field supervisor for Asia, which had opened due to the tragic passing of George Shalm. We were appointed at the general conference in Salt Lake City, Utah, in 1988. We felt privileged to be able to help to spread the gospel and work with so many fine missionary families throughout the countries of Asia. Then in 1994, my husband was appointed as coordinator of overseas ministries at headquarters in St. Louis.

After our return to the United States, our children entered school in St. Louis. While on the field, we were unable to afford the American schools in Islamabad,

Pakistan, and I just couldn't send them to boarding schools. I felt that since the Lord gave them to me, they were my responsibility. I also felt that bestowing our values upon our children was important even though I didn't see how I could make sure they received a good education, since I didn't have a teaching degree. With God's help they have all excelled in spite of me! I need not have been so fearful for them.

Jeffrey graduated *magna cum laude*, third in his class at a college preparatory school. He had scholarships to both Massachusetts Institute of Technology and Worcester Polytechnical Institute. He married a lovely young lady, Laura Jean Fuller, and they spent time in Germany under the AIM program, working with Brother and Sister Arlie Enis in the military work there. During their time in Germany, the Lord called Jeffrey into full-time ministry. He felt it the will of God to accept Charles Clanton's offer to work as his youth minister in Moore, Oklahoma. On October 22, 1996, Jeff and Laura made us grandparents for the first time. Zachary Allan was born and is the light of Nana and Papa's life.

Julie graduated *summa cum laude* with numerous achievement awards, and then she went to the United Pentecostal Bible Institute in New Brunswick, Canada, for two years. There she met her future husband, Peter Wayne Long. They went their third year to Gateway College of Evangelism in St. Louis. Julie worked at World Evangelism Center for the Foreign Missions Division for approximately one and a half years before she and her husband felt a call to serve under the Associates in Missions program in the Caribbean for six months.

During their stay in the islands, Peter interviewed for a ministerial license with the United Pentecostal Church and received a general license. Upon their return to St. Louis, Julie once again began working for the Foreign Missions Division and Peter for the Sunday School Division at World Evangelism Center. They recently have accepted a position as youth pastor and church secretary for the United Pentecostal Church in St. John, New Brunswick, Canada, pastored by Edward Goddard. Both of them feel that somewhere in their future they will once again work on foreign soil.

Joy graduated *cum laude* from Pattonville High School in Maryland Heights, Missouri, and was listed in *Who's Who of American High Schools* for several years. She worked for WAVE Technologies in St. Louis as a customer service manager prior to her wedding on September 27, 1997, to Kevin Michael Brown. Kevin is an electrical engineer working for Korda-Nemeth in Columbus, Ohio, where they are presently living. Joy's dream is one day to be a missionary.

Our children, to this day, still tell us that they wouldn't trade their lives of being brought up on the mission field with any child in America or Canada.

From the time I was a child I always felt a special feeling each time there was a foreign missionary at either our church or camp meeting. I felt so honored just to be in the presence of these people who I felt must be the very elite in God's service. I attended every missionary meeting I could and cried through them all. While I don't consider myself elite, I do still feel honored to be in the presence of other missionaries . . . and I still cry!

Strength and honour are her clothing; and she shall rejoice in time to come (Proverbs 31:25).

CHAPTER 28

Belinda Filkins

SWITZERLAND AND IVORY COAST

I surprised my young Texas parents by arriving a month early. Until the summer I was ten, we lived in Lubbock. It was there, between the ages of four and eight, that I experienced the miracles of provision, healing, and salvation, in that order.

In an Easter revival, I started to the altar to pray, believing Daddy would follow me. He did. Not only was I the first child and granddaughter, I knew I was the apple of his eye. Daddy and I both received the Holy Ghost in that revival. I was baptized in the marvelous name of Jesus the following Sunday in an Easter sunrise service.

At a young age, I determined in my heart that I would always serve God and give Him my best. I also decided that I would marry a preacher. That was almost fifty years ago, and I've never had one moment's regret over those childhood decisions.

When I was twelve, we were in a wonderful church in Tulsa, Oklahoma. A strong emphasis was placed on preaching and teaching the Word, along with prayer, fasting, and missions. We often had missionaries to visit and minister to the church and Christian school. There I learned to fast, asked God to make me an intercessor, and felt a missionary call. Years later God brought it to pass.

As a teenager, after a move from Tulsa back to Arkansas, I renewed my determination to let nothing stand in my way or hinder me from doing God's will in my life. I told the Lord, "If anything seems questionable, I won't chance doing it. I won't risk my walk with You. There isn't anything too big to give up and nothing too hard for me to do, if it's for You."

That commitment kept me safe and on track through many situations in life. Not only was it my life's philosophy and consecration as a young person, I've had several occasions to prove it since.

After I was grown, my family moved to San Jose, California. I stayed in Oklahoma another six months and then joined them. Voar Shoemake was our pastor. I fell in love with Brother and Sister Shoemake, the church, and the people right away.

While attending a Sunday school conference in Fresno, I was introduced to my future husband. He was a Bible instructor and choir director at Western Apostolic Bible College (now Christian Life College) in Stockton. His family had moved from Ohio to San Jose when he was eighteen. He was still a member of the church in San Jose. We were married there fifteen months after meeting, just before our twenty-fifth birthdays.

At the time we got married, my husband was assisting in Pasadena, California. From there we went into full-time evangelistic work. We went from the West Coast to the East Coast, then to the extreme southern tip of Texas, and back to California in one year. During that year, for the most part, we were ministering in small and home missions churches. We did anything and everything we could to help those pastors and churches.

Before pastoring, my husband worked as assistant pastor several times. The highlight experience of all assistantships, was working with O. W. Williams in Houston, Texas (1968-69). That church financed the move to our first pastorate in Grand Junction, Colorado.

Unknown to me, my husband had felt a call to missions in his first year in Bible college. We were pastoring in Marianna, Arkansas, at the time the Lord renewed and defined this call in my husband's heart. Now, after seventeen years of various types of ministerial training and experience, the Lord dealt with him again, saying, "Now, it is time."

Sunday morning church was over. Almost everyone had gone home. I sat down near the back to keep an eye on our girls (ages two, five, and six) while my husband finished talking with a new young couple. I picked up the *Pentecostal Herald* to scan a one-page article by the Foreign Missions Division. It was presented as angels conversing with the Lord, asking, "Who will carry the saving message of Jesus Christ to Switzerland?" It also named some other countries that did not yet have a missionary preaching deliverance, salvation, and healing in the name of Jesus. The angels were offering themselves to go and preach, but Jesus answered, "No, you may not go. This message must be carried on the shoulders of people, people who have experienced redemption."

It seemed that some of the words and one sentence in particular stood out in bold letters, being indelibly imprinted within my heart. The impact was indescribably powerful, yet gentle at the same time. Tears started streaming. I felt almost driven to the floor with the weight of an overwhelming burden.

For several weeks my spirit was infiltrated and frustrated with this burden from which I found no relief. It became an obstinate, ever-growing thing, filling my conscious being. It took precedence over all other subjects of prayer. A very disturbing factor was that while it seemed I could not talk about it, I couldn't concentrate on anything else either. It was a spiritual barricade, impairing my daily communication with Jesus. I'd kneel to pray and sit as though stunned, eventually crying my way through to a deep level of travail, still finding no relief or lifting of the burden. I could find no words to say. I longed for some expression on the subject. I needed clarification. I wanted to, but dared not, talk with anyone else. I had to talk with Jesus first. How could I feel so acutely aware on the one hand and so dead on the other?

Weary of living in the grip of this awesome thing, I finally said to the Lord one day, "Okay, God, I can't go any further like this. We have to talk about it. Why am I afraid to talk about this whole thing and yet I seem unable to speak or even think on any other subject until I do?" Then it clearly came to me, "Because you do not want, nor can you accept, this call unless your husband also has it." Possessing full confidence in God's design and my husband's leadership, I couldn't understand being so mixed up. I wondered, What should I do?

At that point, the Lord reminded me of when I'd just graduated from high school at Apostolic Bible College in Tulsa, Oklahoma. I'd turned sixteen and moved with my family to Fayetteville, Arkansas. Jobs were very hard to find, but I did get one, working part time in The Shoe Store on the square. During that time I took in ironing for several university students and doctors, earning the wonderful wage of seventy-five cents an hour, or fifteen cents per piece. I greatly preferred the latter, since I could iron ten to fifteen shirts an hour. I baby-sat as well. I was diligently saving, as I had been doing all through my high school years. I had two specific goals in mind: I wanted to travel and go to college.

I'd considered the State Teacher's College in Tahlequah, Oklahoma, but decided against it since we had no church there at the time. Then I decided to go to

Western Apostolic Bible College in Stockton, California. Mom helped make a list, and I bought all the linens and things I'd need for my room. Most importantly, I had a ride arranged. As I was telling Daddy this great news, he vetoed the whole plan with one dreadfully cruel, disheartening phrase, "You're just too young to go so far from home." I was sixteen going on twenty-five, but whatever Daddy decided, I accepted.

I don't know if it was taught or caught, but I really believed that "where there's a will, there's a way," and that I could accomplish anything I wanted badly enough. So, unable to go to college while still young, I decided to get a good job. To my dismay, I found that the personnel managers also thought I was too young. The type of job I wanted, such as working as a legal or medical secretary, was not yet available to me. All I knew to do was just keep working and hope and pray that my whole life would not waste away before ever being able to do anything important!

Since the age of eight, I'd been set on marrying a preacher. At fifteen, I fell in love at first sight with and later dated a young man who was a wonderful evangelist. A couple of years later when the question of marriage came up, I too felt that I was too young.

Unexpectedly, came the chance of a lifetime! A wealthy couple I baby-sat for offered to sponsor me to study abroad. I knew immediately that Switzerland was my number-one choice. It seemed a dream too good to be true, but it was really happening. I wanted to jump at this unbelievably awesome opportunity and clinch the idea, but I asked the Rogerses, "Please wait and let me pray and talk to my parents about this. I'll let you know next Friday night if I can accept." What exhilaration and anxious joy I felt! My life was finally coming together. The wonderful and worthwhile goals I'd so wanted to accomplish were in sight—not impossible after all!

I felt extremely grateful and happy. In prayer, I rejoiced

and then agonized, realizing that in order to fulfill it, I'd have to leave family and church involvement behind. I could not afford such a great price. I softly laid my dream-hope to rest with the Lord. Going to college in Switzerland was a desirable jewel, but keeping my consecration vow was more precious to me. I chose to keep the vow.

Years later, in Marianna, Arkansas, as I was kneeling at the couch with our baby girl on my lap, it all came into focus. As soon as I'd said I had to talk to God about Switzerland, I immediately felt assurance. The intense stress of the weeks of stony silence began to fall away, as understanding and enlightenment replaced the fears and disappointment that had plagued me for so long. I told Jesus, "The reason for not going before has all changed. If I go now to Switzerland as a missionary, I'd have my husband-pastor, my family, and a church, in time." In wonder and joy I exclaimed, "Lord, You are giving my abandoned dream back to me . . . with interest! How marvelous! Yes, Jesus, if that's what You have in mind, I gladly accept!"

What relief, what calm, what peace now prevailed. The tears began to flow, pure liquid joy. The atmosphere was sweet and uncomplicated. Then began a consistent pondering, awe, and anticipation, waiting for Him to bring it to pass. While it seemed that my whole reason for being had changed, deep down inside I realized that He was only continuing what He had started in my heart at the tender age of eight.

I started rereading *Heidi*, *Jorli*, and any other stories I found in the setting of the majestic Alps. I ordered slides of the Swiss ski slopes to show the girls. While I was happy just savoring this beautiful secret that I knew God would surely bring to pass one day, the Lord was also dealing with my dear husband, bringing back and renewing the missionary call he'd felt seventeen years earlier, during his first year at WABC.

I don't know how much time passed with this burden in our hearts and uppermost in our minds before either of us mentioned it. I had made sure any remarks about shared pictures and so on were very general.

One bright sunny morning, not long after the conversation between the Lord and me, I met Robert on the stairway as he was going to the library. To my knowledge, that was rare behavior for him! When he told me that he was looking for information on Switzerland, my heart leaped and then stood ever so still. At that moment, standing on the stairway, he broke the news to me: "How would you feel if I told you I'm called to be a missionary?"

My pent-up female emotions caused the waterworks to start. He then began trying to comfort me about leaving my parents and the emotional upheaval he knew it would cause to take their three precious granddaughters to a foreign country. He added, apologetically, "I don't want to take you and the girls so far away from your mom and dad, but I feel it so strongly."

I managed to get enough emotional control to say, "These are tears of *joy*, not sorrow." I then gladly admitted, "The Lord has also been dealing with me about Switzerland."

From that day forward, Switzerland became a household word. Getting to be missionaries was the focus of our conversation at work, meals, play, and especially prayer time. We must have thought about it in our sleep. We never mentioned it at church, but nobody had said not to. We really didn't want to tell our congregation anything until we'd met the Foreign Missions Board and had something to tell.

One Sunday morning, coming out of the class of four- and five-year-olds, the teacher said to me, "Are ya'll going to be missionaries?"

I cautiously replied with a question of my own, "Sister Velma, why do you ask?"

"Well" she replied, "we studied about missions today, and Dionna tells us ya'll are going to Switzerland to be missionaries. Is that true?"

I stuttered a moment, "Uh, I think, uh, you should talk to my husband about it." I was quite flustered, but I knew enough to make a beeline to inform him of what was coming! We knew we didn't have anything official to announce, but he did talk to the church that night about the feeling in our hearts, asking them to pray with us about it.

Little did we then understand just how long the road to getting an appointment can be. Our church understood even less of the missions process. When we procured an appointment to meet the Foreign Missions Board at the next general conference, being green and naïve, we believed that was all there was to it. I guess it is called blissful ignorance.

That was the only blissful element, however. Pain was poignant, as we empathized with our precious people. They went through all the normal feelings of abandonment, rejection, and fears of letting us go, before reaching a level of acceptance. They loved us as strongly as we did them, and we all suffered at the thought of separation, but they finally became glad to have a part in God's greater plan.

For two years our family was totally absorbed with the idea of going to Switzerland. We carefully took every step, as directed. After filling out applications, getting recommendations, and passing medical examinations and various boards, we could not begin to describe the shock we felt upon learning we were not appointed! Rejected? Impossible! Surely, there was some mistake!

A kaleidoscope of questions assaulted us. In the missions service the foreign missions director made a passionate appeal for "men who'll give themselves, for people with a burden who will answer the Macedonian call." It was said, "We have the money, we need *men*. Who will respond to the powerful Spirit that now hovers here over us all?"

We were crushed. Broken and sobbing, we made our

way to join the others pouring into the altar. Never in my entire life was I so confused. We knew we'd heard from God. Could we have imagined this call of God on our lives? No, this burden could not have been conjured up any more than it could be waved away with a magic wand. "Please, God. I don't mean to question You or Your will, but where do we go from here?" I'll be forever grateful to the kindhearted board members and the regional field supervisor-to-be who came and prayed for us. We were given wise counsel, although our bruised and broken hearts could not absorb it until some healing time had passed.

We returned to the church in Marianna to give it our best. They were equally surprised and grateful to have us back. During the following year, God graciously gave us additional confirmation of our calling. That gave us hope and courage to meet the board again.

There is more to the story, but suffice it to say that our appointment to Switzerland at the following general conference in Anaheim, California, made us exceedingly happy. Our projected eighteen months of deputational travel was completed in only ten. We had a happy time traveling from church to church in forty-six states and three provinces of Canada. It was also a wonderful educational experience for our girls.

The Lord arranged for our acceptance and early entrance in the missionary language-training school called Le Centre Missionaire. While attending the ten-month course, we founded an infant church in Geneva, Switzerland. The first services started in a living room, with people from three prayer and Bible study groups that another couple had begun. That group of people with diverse cultural and social backgrounds was melded by the handiwork of God into a strong Jesus Name church. It was a thing of beauty to behold their intense prayer and sincere worship. Since our departure, it has become an independent church, registered as The United Pentecostal

Church of Switzerland. At our last contact, they had about five hundred in attendance. Our phone call was answered in the midst of an apostolic prayer meeting!

Just as we were ready to move to Switzerland, our resident visas were blocked. We had the work permits so we applied for French visas, hoping to live in France and work in Geneva. We were told that our papers would be ready in four to twelve weeks. However, after hanging in limbo for a year, we volunteered to go to Ivory Coast, West Africa, as there was a desperate need for someone who could speak French. Not long after arriving, our French visas came through. Too late! We were already committed.

There had been some previous contacts and ground work, but we became the first resident United Pentecostal missionaries in French West Africa. There were miracles, signs, and wonders along with terror, physical attacks, trauma, and health failure. In a little over two years, 967 were baptized, and 650 received the Holy Ghost. To God be the glory!

Our next four years was spent in Trinity, Texas, where the Lord gave us a wonderful group of people to pastor. It was a time of healing and renewal.

The call to foreign missions again prevailed, and we returned to France in February 1985 with three teenage daughters. Pastor Nowacki and the saints in Melun gave us a beautiful welcome and much assistance during our time of adjustment and settling in. While attending language refresher classes, we were privileged to baptize several people as a result of Maleah's teaching *Search for Truth* to a fellow missionary student.

Many changes for our family came during the four and a half years in France. My dad passed on to be with the Lord, and Maleah and Dionna left home for Bible college in California. We missed the girls, both in the home and the church work, but for fifteen-year-old Sherilyn the loneliness was acute. We had moved to Bordeaux to open a new region of France, and the nearest fellowship was a six-hour drive. We also ministered on occasions in Belgium, Italy, Holland, Spain, and the Military District in Germany. On our departure from Bordeaux, the beautifully restored, antique building and church we'd started were turned over to a young French pastor and his American wife. They are doing a wonderful job.

Three months prior to completing deputational travel, at the request of Foreign Missions Division we went for one year to Ivory Coast, to take care of Bible school training and fill in during the absence of Brother and Sister Allard, while they traveled on deputation.

On returning to United States, we resumed our deputational travel for France. In a routine medical checkup, some conditions of a serious nature were discovered. I had some time out for treatment. We passed some uncertain days, wondering if we would be allowed to return to the mission field. God's mercy and the prayers of His people lifted me. The doctor did release me, writing a letter to the Foreign Missions Board.

Now, once again, the Lord put another unexpected turn in our highway of life! Instead of returning to France, for which we'd prayed, planned, and prepared for so long, we went back to Africa! Understand? No. Disappointed? Yes. Trust my husband's decision? By faith, yes. Trust the Lord's leading? With all my heart!

I was filled with shock and sorrow. Sorrow, not so much for going to Africa, as not going to Strasbourg, France! In seeking the Lord's leading, that's the city He'd placed on our hearts as a target. Much prayer preparation was already invested. Now it seemed that this vision, too, was aborted, along with longtime hopes and dreams. I still had thoughts and feelings that had to be emptied out in tearful prayers in order to let the new ones surface. I did not understand, but when my crying was over, I was filled with renewed hope. We went forward in His strength. I just kept holding to His hand.

As we look at the route the Lord used to take the Israelites from Egypt to Canaan, we see many twists and turns, backtracking and delays. They did arrive. Those who hadn't murmured were allowed to pass into the Promised Land. My life has also had its share of disappointing turns, frustrations, and barricades along the way. People make mistakes, humans fail, we struggle, we stumble, we falter. My trust is in the One who's leading me. He has promised victory. I've crossed deep rivers, and I've climbed rugged mountains. When my time comes to cross over, by His grace, through faith, I expect to be found acceptable in His eyes. I'll hear Him say, "Well done," and joyfully enter in.

This time, when we went to Ivory Coast, it was not just on a temporary or fill-in basis. I was willing and ready to do whatever my husband wished and needed me to do. However, I believed that the wife role would be the only one I could fill, with prayer support being my only participation in the work. Since the age of twelve, I'd been very involved in church work, and one of the sacrificial parts of my consecration to go back to Ivory Coast had been to become willing not to do things. Anyway, I decided I'd be the most supportive, content, and happy wife any missionary man had ever had.

A host of Ivorians, along with Brother and Sister Allard, welcomed us at the airport in Abidjan. Since the Bible school classes had begun a few days prior to our arrival, it seemed that my husband hit the ground running while I started learning to cope with leisure time. I actually grew tired of reading.

During the two and a half months it took to rent a house and get our shipment released, we stayed with Allards. They are hospitable and congenial, and made us comfortable. They helped us find a nice house at an unbelievable price. I was elated! It had been five years since we'd had our own home. Discovering all the forgotten stuff and putting it in housekeeping order was great fun.

We certainly had not expected such a large, nice house, but we appreciate and enjoy it very much.

The first few weeks were occupied with the process of settling in. Soon afterward, doors to various avenues of service began to open to me. One, which I felt to be a unique privilege, was teaching new converts in French. I was also invited to help my husband with the Bible school choir classes. I loved doing that. Sister Allard and I worked together on clothing distribution for our pastors and their families. We also organized a fundraiser for home missions, sewing and selling school uniforms.

There were fifty-five churches in the Ivory Coast. Fifteen of those were in the city, but none in our area. In a joint effort, we and the Allards started a new church in our community, shortly before they left for deputation. During their absence I became the ladies leader. We conducted outreach visitation, prayer meetings, teaching sessions, and singings. Many of the ladies do not have money for transportation, so we started regional ladies rallies.

I was thrilled at how easy it is to get both African and expatriate visitors to come to church. I met and made friends with people of every strata of society. From little beggar ladies and children on the street to people in high positions, they all need to know Jesus as their personal friend and Savior. Introducing them fills me with unspeakable joy!

Then came the day I had to return to the United States for required physical exams. I was not overly concerned about taking a three-week medical leave, as my husband is very self-sufficient. I had an unpleasant surprise when the tests showed that I needed a four- or five-bypass heart surgery. I also had an infected bone (left over from a staph infection I had in 1994) removed from my foot. Had it not been for the excellent podiatrist the Lord led us to, I could very well have lost most of my foot. Jesus does all things well.

I didn't like the interruption of my lifestyle and even

less being separated from my husband, but it would have been worse to be defeated. We are, at present, again traveling among our churches in America, finding people who will help us shine the glorious gospel light in French West Africa by investing prayer and finance. We plan to return as soon as possible. We have seen the plentiful harvest, ripe and ready for the reaping.

"They that sow in tears shall reap in joy and singing. He who goes forth, bearing precious seed and weeping (at needing his precious supply of grain for sowing) shall doubtless come again with rejoicing, bringing his sheaves with him" (Psalm 126:5-6, Amplified).

We'll pray and work, we'll go and give,
As long as we have life to live.
Then we'll meet Jesus in His home
And cast our crowns before His throne.

Strength and honour are her clothing; and she shall rejoice in time to come (Proverbs 31:25).

Ladies prayer and visitation group.

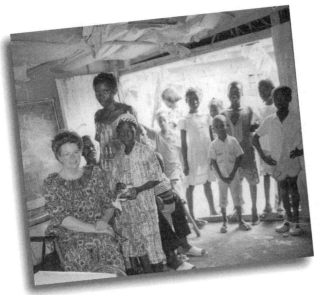

*Left to right: Belinda, guest of honor; teacher;
schoolmaster's daughter; spectators to see the
d'ou ba bou (white woman).*

*This
kindergarten,
first- and
second- grade
class is held in
a construction of
black plastic
bags on the
outside and
cardboard boxes
on the inside.*

*Ladies project:
school dress exposition.*

*Ladies offering dance at headquarters church, Bible school
graduation, 1995. Sister Filkins and oldest daughter are at
front left. Dale taught Bible classes, Maleah translated, and
Gramma baby-sat grandsons.*

CHAPTER 29

Janet Howard

BRAZIL

My dad received the Holy Ghost when I was nine months old. Since my mom was already a Christian, I was fortunate to be raised in a Christian home.

When I was fourteen years old, we were in a tent revival. One night I was worshiping in the Spirit when I suddenly had a vision of myself under a tree teaching some dark-skinned people. I knew from that moment that I would someday be a missionary. At the time, most of the lady missionaries I knew of were single, so I just assumed I would never marry. Anyway, the last thing in the world I ever wanted to be was a minister's wife, so I fully intended to stay single.

When I turned sixteen, I met Frank Howard. The first night he walked into our church was during a revival. He had been at work and didn't arrive until 11 P.M. On his second visit, he received the Holy Ghost, and we became friends. In spite of my determination to remain single, I became serious about Frank, even sooner than he did about me.

My dad was a lay minister in our local church. One day, the pastor spoke to him of the need for someone to go to Manaus, Brazil, to help two single missionary ladies. My mom was willing to go, so we all went. I was eighteen at the time and was upset at the thought of leaving Frank.

When my family went to New York to prepare to go to Brazil, Frank came to see me while on leave from the army. After boot camp, he would be leaving for Vietnam to serve as a medic. I was so happy to see him! My parents were going to the church service, but I felt too sick and stayed in bed. Frank volunteered to stay with my sister and me while they were gone. He soon diverted my sister by asking her to make us some popcorn. Then he asked me if I would marry him. My carefully laid "single missionary" plans went right out the window, and my recovery was remarkably quick!

We were separated for fifteen months while I went to Brazil and he went to Vietnam. My sister didn't like Manaus, Brazil, at all and once told my dad that the Lord had said, "*My house*, not *Manaus*." We had been there one year when my mom became very ill with yellow fever, which was not uncommon in that equatorial jungle area. Due to her extreme illness, we had to return to the United States. A few months later, Frank returned from Vietnam, and three months later we were married.

Frank had been raised in a different religion but had always felt that he would someday be a missionary. However, he was not even a preacher, and I certainly was never going to be the wife of a minister. So I didn't take his call seriously.

After his discharge from the military, we moved to Tulsa, Oklahoma. He began working at various positions in the church and in the church school, and occasionally he preached mini-sermons. He gradually increased his preaching and was invited to preach at other churches. As his ministry began to unfold, I gradually accepted that I had indeed married a preacher!

One night, my husband had a dream that he was lying down in a wheatfield with his hands behind his head looking at the beautiful blue sky overhead when the Lord spoke to him, "When a certain missionary writes and says they are coming home from the field, prepare yourself to go to Brazil."

The following day, he saw the pastor's wife and told her about the dream. She looked startled and said, "Brother Howard, I received a letter from them this morning, and they are coming home."

When he came home and told me of the dream and the letter, my response was, "Then, we will have to sell everything we have and get ready to go." It seemed very natural to me, and I was willing to go.

At that time, we were in an independent church. We were only sponsored by our local church and had to raise our funds the best way we could.

While I was totally willing to follow my husband and do what I could to support him in the ministry and in fulfilling his call to the foreign field, I had, nonetheless, some terrible battles over having to sell and give away some of my wedding presents. We had been married only five years, and I was thoroughly enjoying my home, especially my kitchen. I could still remember who had given me what. To sell the presents, which were so precious to me, in order to raise our necessary money, caused many tears. Even more difficult than parting with my own beloved articles was having to part with my children's baby clothes and toys. I especially remember my daughter as she chased someone down the sidewalk crying, "Mommy, Mommy, that's my doll. Don't let them take my doll." Although we kept what we possibly could of their belongings, there was just no way we could keep them all. Things like this *really* brought the tears; we *all* cried.

I have always been an extremely shy person, which has caused me a few problems. When we would go to preach for other churches in hopes of raising some funds, I was always so nervous that I often had my husband circle around the block many times before I could get the courage to go in. He got used to me saying, "Just once more around the block, honey, just once more."

By the time we left for Brazil, our daughter, Tonja, was three years old, and our son, Kevin, was eleven months.

I had liked living in Manaus, even though it was primitive and was in the middle of the Amazon jungle. When my husband, children, and I went to the city of Campinas, in the state of San Paulo, it was so modern compared to Manaus that I didn't feel that I had returned to Brazil at all. I didn't feel that I was a real missionary, because I wasn't suffering or feeling deprived of necessities.

After spending time in Brazil as independent missionaries, we later returned to the United States and attended a United Pentecostal church. We were eventually appointed as United Pentecostal missionaries. I will probably always be shy, but deputational travel doesn't leave much spare time, so I finally had to stop asking Frank to circle the block.

Even though we have faced many difficulties on the field, I have never doubted our call. Being convinced that the Bible teaches that the man is the head of the house and therefore the one responsible for the final decisions concerning a family, has relieved me of a great deal of pressure. He was to lead; I was to follow and trust God to give us reliable directions.

In spite of many problems and hardships, I do not regret our decision to come to Brazil. We have three children, and they are all still doing their best to serve God. Tonja is now married, has two children, and they are living in the United States. Janita is married to a Brazilian, lives in the United States, and has given us two grandchildren. Kevin is also married. He, too, lives in the United States but has at times returned to Brazil to preach through the AIM program.

I realize that missionary kids often have terrific problems, and mine have certainly had their share. I also am aware that some missionary kids backslide. But I don't for a minute believe that this is a result of their parents following God to a far country. Many parents have refused to go to a foreign field because of their children and have eventually lost them, even though they stayed in the United States. Others, ministers and laymen alike, who were never called to go to another country, have raised their children in the best of homes, schools, neighborhoods, and churches but have also had children become rebellious and give them all kinds of problems. While we can never know what reaction and decisions our children will make, the environment inside the home is more important than the one outside the home. The safest place to raise children is in the will of God, whether that be at home or abroad.

The Howards went to the field when their children were babies. After twenty-one years in Brazil, the Lord has brought them back to the United States, where they are working to build a home missions church in Long Beach, California, as well as pastoring in Van Nuys, California.

Her children arise up, and call her blessed; her husband also, and he praiseth her (Proverbs 31:28).

CHAPTER 30

Carol Rash

INDONESIA, AUSTRIA, HOLLAND, AND GERMANY

The first and shocking call came at the general conference in Salt Lake City in 1973. Brother and Sister George White were standing on the platform along with all the other missionaries during the Sunday foreign missions service. They were weeping because they wanted to return to Indonesia, but they were not reappointed due to their age. (Brother White was then seventy-two years old.) Then came a message in tongues and interpretation saying, "Who will take the place of the man with the white hair? Do I not have a man that will fill in the gap?"

Such a heavy spirit of weeping and concern came over the whole congregation! I noticed that my husband stood to his feet, and then I noticed others standing and weeping also. My husband began to cry, almost out of control, and he continued to weep through the entire service. I knew that God was calling him to Indonesia, but I was asking in my mind, Where in all of God's green earth is Indonesia?

It is true, though, that ever since I was a very young girl, I thought that I would like to be a missionary. I loved subjects like social studies and world geography in school. I took two years of Spanish in high school, thinking I might go to Latin America as a missionary someday.

I began attending Bible college in Stockton, California, which was also my hometown and church. My husband was saved there also and began Bible college. That is where we began dating. We were married in 1958 right after his graduation from Bible college.

Only one month after our marriage, we went to Coolidge, Arizona, to work with the Pima Indians on the Sacaton Reservation. We also went to help in the home missions work in Coolidge. This was excellent missionary experience for us. Our first child was born in a little county hospital there in the desert.

Later we came back to Stockton, where our second child was born. We were shocked to learn that he was born with a hole in his heart. When he was two years old, little Jonathan had to have open-heart surgery and the Lord miraculously healed him. Through this experience, we learned a lot about trusting the Lord in every circumstance.

During the next three years, we stayed in Stockton and assisted Clyde J. Haney in the church. My husband was the Sunday school superintendent, and we worked with the youth and young married couples.

In 1963, my husband got a job for the state of California in Sacramento, and there we assisted Pastor Riddlesperger in the church in Carmichael. We were there five and a half years, and our last two children were born during that time. My husband's ministry really began to develop as he served as youth leader and assistant pastor. Many young people came into the church during that time who are ministers and even missionaries today.

In 1969, my husband often drove through the small mountain town of Grass Valley, California, on his way to visit his mother. He kept saying that he would love to start a church that preached the full gospel in that town. By July of that same year, we had moved to Grass Valley to begin a home missions work. We didn't know one person in that town when we moved there, but God was in it, and He blessed us in wonderful ways. Through His help, we were able to build a beautiful new church building, along with a lovely congregation that is still continuing to do well today.

We were pastoring in Grass Valley when we decided to go to the 1973 conference in Salt Lake City. We left the children with a baby-sitter, and during the drive there, my husband told me that he felt that God was going to tell him where we were to serve God overseas. He had felt for several years that we would be going into foreign missionary service. But where and when?

After that outstanding missionary service on Sunday, Brother Rash felt a definite call and burden for Indonesia. We decided to keep it totally to ourselves for the next two months. We seldom even spoke of it to each other. We wanted to be sure that it was really from the Lord and not just from being in an emotional missionary service. During the next two months, I secretly began to read up on the country of Indonesia, and the more I read about it, the less I wanted to go. I read about hot humid jungles, mosquitoes, fevers, Muslims, and many languages, just to name a few of the discouraging factors involved. I also learned that I would have to teach all four of my children, as there were no English schools where we would be.

I prayed many days and wept before the Lord in the privacy of my home, asking God not to let us go if it was not His perfect will for us.

I was the baby of seven children, and I hated even to think of leaving my elderly mother behind, especially after the recent loss of my father and oldest brother. My mother seemed to depend on me so much.

Two months after that great missionary service in Salt Lake City, my husband came in from work and said, "The burden has not left me, and I feel the same about going to Indonesia. Go ahead and write headquarters and ask for an application form."

It took one full year of sending forms back and forth to the Foreign Missions Division. Then came the appointment to meet the board in Louisville, Kentucky, in 1974. Of course, we were scared to death, as most young couples are when they meet the board for the first time. I have found, however, that we had nothing to fear. The people of the Foreign Missions Division are some of the best friends we could ever have.

We were approved to go to Indonesia and went directly home to resign our church. Then we went straight to the School of Missions. Things had to move very quickly then. (We did not resign our church or tell anyone about our plans until we got the approval from the board. This waiting is important in order to prevent the undoing of plans made prematurely.)

We then sold our home and bought a motor home. We traveled for the next ten months with all four of our children. I could write a very interesting book about the deputational trail! We traveled many miles singing with our children, "We all live in a green motor home."

I had mixed emotions about going to a country like Indonesia. Indonesia is just below Vietnam and Cambodia. Back in 1974, it was still a war-torn area. There were a lot of questions and fears in my heart and mind. Could I learn a new language? Would my children be able to adjust to a Third World country? Would we get sick with malaria and other jungle fevers? What kind of house would we live in—or would I even have a house? Could I teach my four children with their varying ages? Would we be terribly lonely?

All I can say now, these many years later, is, Yes, I

could learn even three foreign languages. Yes, I could teach my children until we moved to a place that had a school. Yes, we could survive having malaria and dengue fever and amoebae. Yes, the Lord would sustain us through any lonely hours that we might have. And, yes, we really could adjust to a whole new world.

Now we've been in Indonesia, Austria, Holland, and Germany. Each country has its own culture shock. I suffered as much of a shock going to Vienna, Austria, as I did in arriving in Java, Indonesia. Every country has its own set of problems and blessings as well. There is a positive and negative side to almost everything. We must look for the positive!

One thing is sure: *God is faithful,* and He will never forsake us!

No, I did not receive my own personal call to be a missionary, but my call came years ago when I said, "I do," at a wedding altar.

The Lord brought them back from the mission field and Brother and Sister Rash are now living in Stockton, California, where they are very active in Bro. Haney's Asian church.

Not that I speak in respect of want: for I have learned, in whatsoever state I am, therewith to be content. I can do all things through Christ which strengtheneth me (Philippians 4:11, 13).

Brother and Sister Rash singing in Melun, France, 1982.

Sister Rash with an Indonesian lady.

Sister Rash in church with her two youngest children, Medan, Sumatra, Indonesia, 1979.

*But now they desire a
better country, that is, an heavenly:
wherefore God is not ashamed to be
called their God: for he hath
prepared for them a city*
(Hebrews 11:16).

CHAPTER 31

The Diversity of Sarah's Daughters

by Bonnie Markham

As you can observe from the numerous examples in this book, you do not have to be from a "correct" family or background. When God calls you to work for Him, He is aware of your relationship with your family, your background, your faults, and your most humiliating failures. When He chooses you to do a task for Him, it is because He has found some unique quality in you that He needs in a certain place at a certain time.

Sarah was "on the field" for sixty-two years and is a tremendous example to all women, especially ministers' wives, whether they be pastors, evangelists, or home or foreign missionaries. In spite of her tremendous contribution, almost all that is ever spoken of Sarah is her anger at Hagar and that she doubted God. Once! Only in regard to doubting that she could conceive a child after she reached age seventy-five did Sarah ever falter. Dare we criticize?

Just as her error has become spotlighted, perhaps some of these ladies, or even members of their families, have made errors, possibly only once, that have become subjected to the bright glare of light, leaving years of faithfulness and productivity in the shadows to be mentioned rarely. Jesus revealed that each of us has sinned. Dare we criticize one another? Repentance is part of God's plan and available to all. God told Peter not to call common or unclean anything He has cleansed. It would be frightening to judge any person as being common or unclean if he has sincerely repented and God has cleansed him with His blood. Thank God for the blood! Whatever may or may not be in the lives of these ladies or their families, I pray that each will, in the end, be victorious over all. I salute their efforts!

Many missionary wives received their experience through the most difficult of all training schools—home missions! The many defeats, sacrifices, struggles, stresses, and sometimes dull drudgery involved in digging out a church on home soil usually weeds out the fainthearted. Any who have waded through *that* battlefield, and can still raise their hands to volunteer for the foreign field, must have an awesome desire and determination to do something for God. Not all passed through that particular fire *before* going to the field; some were willing to become home missionaries *after* foreign service.

If you want to find a genuine daughter of Sarah, you don't have to leave your country. Look at the women struggling to do and be something for God in our small churches. Thankfully, many have helped their small church become a large one, and they have sacrificed much in the process.

To all women, whether part of the ministry or members who are remaining faithful and continuing to follow God in small churches and large, on the field or at home, win or lose, sink or swim, I believe in you and cherish you as my sister. Just as Sarah was mentioned in the roll call of the faithful in Hebrews 11, so was Rahab the harlot. God is not as concerned with where you came from as He is with where you are willing to be sent. Perhaps the Lord wants to send you to your neighbor next door, to a co-worker, or to a home missions work—the greatest proving ground there is. All that remains is for you to respond, "Here am I, Lord; send me."

Hearken, O daughter, and consider, and incline thine ear; forget also thine own people, and thy father's house; so shall the king greatly desire thy beauty: for he is thy Lord; and worship thou him. The king's daughter is all glorious within. . . . With gladness and rejoicing shall they be brought: they shall enter into the king's palace (Psalm 45:10-15).

Hearken to me, ye that follow after righteousness, ye that seek the LORD: look unto the rock whence ye are hewn, and to the hole of the pit whence ye are digged. Look . . . unto Sarah that bare you (Isaiah 51:1-2).

Not unto us, O Lord, *not unto us, but unto thy name give glory, for thy mercy, and for thy truth's sake* (Psalm 115:1).

Appendix
Missionary Women

The following are names of ladies who are serving, or have served, as missionaries with the United Pentecostal Church International. Some ladies served on the mission field with the Pentecostal Assemblies of Jesus Christ or the Pentecostal Church Incorporated before the two merged to become the United Pentecostal Church. Any omissions of past or present missionary ladies are unintentional. There are also ladies of other groups who have gone overseas to proclaim the great truth of the gospel, whose names are not available to us. God knows each one, and He will reward each according to His records.

Lori Aber
Janet Abernathy
Miriam Abernathy
Sharon Abernathy
Ferne Scism Ackley
Carolyn Adams
Evelyn Adams
Judy Anne Addington
Amelia Allard
Elizabeth Andrade
Kathleen Arcidiacono
Dorothy Arthur
Dollyne Asarisi
Geneva Bailey
Janice M. Bain

Lois Baker
Renee Baker
Ruth Baker
Jeannie Baker
Patricia Balca
Grace Ball
Jeanne Banta
Maurine Barcus
Nellie Barley
Mary Bash
Clairee Battle
Mary Baumeister
Mrs. Paul Bayne
Sue Beasley
Judy Bentley

Carolyn Berglund
Loretta Bernard
Edith R. Berthoux
Maurine Bettis
Loretta Bir
Janet Black
Mrs. James R. Blackshear
Jeanine Blake
Ruth Blake
Pat Blunt
Madeline Iris Bogue
Brenda Boller
Evelyn Bolton
Ella Borders
Sandra Bracken
Madeline Brian
Terry Brian
Darla Brochu
Kathy Brott
Lolita Brown
Rosa Browne
Donna Bryant
Ellen Buck
Joyce Buck
Becky Buckland
Hettie Irene Buckmiller
Mrs. Ralph Bullock
Patricia Burgess
Kay Burgess
Beverly Burk
Beth Burns
Margaret Burns
Gail Burton
Martha Burton
Vivian Caffee
Bobbie Carpenter
Nancy Carpenter

Barbara Carr
Kay Carter
Margaret Carver
Mrs. E. W. Caughron
Annette Chelette
Brenda Ciulla
Beverly Clark
Pearl Clark
Virginia Clark
Linda Clenney
Marilee Clonch
Rhoda Cobb
Antonina Cogan
Shirley Cole
Winona Cole
Bonnie Laverne Collins
Cynthia Collins
Jean Collins
Rebecca Collins
Faith Cook
Pearl Cooper
Esther Coote
Lois Corcoran
Connie Corney
Effie Crackel
Cheryl Craft
Kathy Crossley
Karen Crumpacker
Maxine Cunningham
Sharon Cruz
Francis Cupples
Deborah Curtis
Bernice Davis
Mary Davis
Norma Davis
Virginia Davis
Joy Dawson

Theresa DeMerchant

Valerie Demos

Shirley Dennis

Coral Denny

Eleanor Roberta Dillon

Sister Dixon

Angela Doan

Martha Dobyns

Eva Domingues

Billie Dotson

Roxie Artelie Dover

Jennifer Downey

Danita Drost

Holley Drost

Susan Drost

Ruth Drost

Wanda Drost

Carol Duke

Evelyn Dykes

Robbie Eaton

Marilyn Edge

Sandi Edmonds

Ruth Edwards

Becki Enis

Carrie Eastridge

Lucille Farmer

Belinda Filkins

Suzanne Fitch

Barbara Flannery

Donna Flowers

Derethia Forbush

Francis Foster

Nona Freeman

Gayle Frizzell

Mary French

Peggy Garrison

Hazel Gee

Donna Geissler

Mozelle Gerald

Eva Glaser

Darlene Goodwin

Catherine Grant

Mrs. Gray

Rita Green

Esther Grimm

Rachel Grissom

Patricia Grosbach

Pauline Gruse

Edna Hall

Patricia Hall

Glida Hampton

Esther Haney

Joy Hanscom

Saundra Hanscom

Elly Hansen

Barbara Edwards Hanson

Linda Hare

Ellie Harris

Rachel Hattabaugh

Diana Hayes

Katherine Hendricks

Esther Henry

Mabel Hensley

Brenda Hill

Donna Holland

Joan Holland

Verda Holley

Pearl Holmes

Fayetta Holt

Aletha Hoover

Aurelia Hopkins

Janet Howard

Diane Howell

Mrs. John Huba

Phyliss Huerta
June Hughes
Mrs W. L. Hull
Betty Hyde
Ena Hylton
Elizabeth Ikerd
Sharon Ikerd
Mrs. P. Ireland
Mae Iry
Mrs. Peter Isaac
Mrs. Samuel Jensen
Lynne Jewett
Helen Johnson
Martha Johnson
Pat Johnson
Shirley Johnson
Eleanor Johnston
Evelyn Judd
Cammy Kondas
Jerolyn Kelley
Della Mae Kennedy
Cathy Killoren
Ey Ja Kim
Mary Kinney
Pamela Kirk
Ruby Klemin
Alice Kline
Sibyl Krause
Jeri Lafferty
Mrs. J. B. Lambeth
Kristi Landaw
Suzanna Lang
Sandra Langham
Bonnie Langley
Fayetta Larsen
Nancy Lassetter
Joyce Latta

Alice Leaman
Sallie Lemons
Darlene Lewis
Donna Lewis
Rosemary Louw
Jean Lucas
Else Lund
Raymonde Mahautiere
Afton Mallory
Treva Manuwal
Bonnie Markham
Angela Marquez
Henrietta Marquez
Patricia Anne Marshall
Jo Ann Marshall
Mrs. Martinez
Geneva Mason
Suzana Mathiasz
Marcena May
Mother D. L. McCarty
Bonnie McCrury
Marjorie McFarland
Dorothy McGaha
Jo Ann McGriffin
Lynda McIntyre
Phebe McInnerney
Chris McQuay
Janeace Miller
Kathy L. Miller
Marilyn Miller
Mrs. John Mogg
Sofia Monday
Loretta Moreau
Sallie Morley
Helen Moulton
Myrtle Mowatt
Frances Munsey

Martha Myre
Sandra Nepstad
Judith Nicholls
Corinne Nickerson
Ester Nigh
Corliss Nilsen
Kathy Nix
Sue Nix
Valerie Nix
Wilma Ruth Nix
Yvonne Nix
Eunice Norris
Ivana Norris
Jean Norris
Judy Norris
Anne Nowacki
Teri O'Daniel
Lynnette O'Donnell
Abigail O'Keefe
Jane Olson
Erma Owens
Sallie Pardue
Dorothy Parks
Dianne Parsons
Euna Patrick
Mary Patridge
Myrtle J. Patrick
Valita Jean Patterson
Barbara Peavy
Connie Pennington
Mary Perdue
Clara Peterson
Nancy Petty
Roselle Petty
Nancy Plowman
Linda Poitras
Christine Pool

Karen Poole
Patricia Porter
Mrs. A. W. Post
Linda Potter
Wanda Price
Mrs. Wesley Priest
Marilyn Pruett
Charlotte Purcell
Susie Raimond
Thada Raley
Jeanne Ramsey
Carol Rash
Linda Reed
Shelba Reed
Georgia Regenhardt
Beth Reynolds
Helen Reynolds
Willie Mae Reynolds
Faith Reznicsek
Sandra Rhodes
Agnes Rich
Alice Rich
Freida Richardson
Paula Richardson
Theresa Richardson
Vickie Richardson
Cheryl Riddick
Sharon Ritchie
Joyce Rivers
Teresa Roberts
Carol Robertson
Gladys Robinson
Dorothy Roca
Evangeline Rodenbush
Mary Roh
Geneva Mason Rose
Darlene Kantola Royer

Brenda Russell
Valda Russell
Joan Wiseman Sandburg
Brenda Sawyer
Judy Schreckhise
Lycia Schreckhise
Yonda Schwarz
Audrene Scism
Marjorie Scism
Joretta Scott
Lane Scott
Millie Scott
Vida Scott
Mary Seay
Teresa Sedra
Myra Seymour
Georgene Shalm
Kathy Shalm
Margaret Shalm
Dian Sharp
Elli Sharp
Era Belle Shaw
Alice Sheets
Bonnie Sheets
Becky Sherry
Karin Shirley
Nancy Shirley
Helen Shoemaker
Dianne Showalter
Betty Shrum
Robin Shutes
Suzanna Sikora
Carolyn Simoneaux
Vickie Simoneaux
Krista Slaydon
Ida Sly
Ruth Sly

Delta Smith
Leah Smith
Rachel Smith
Vickie Smith
Pam Smoak
Melva Sones
Loice Sparks
Miriam Sponsler
Mariann Starin
Josephine Starks
Madeline Rose Steeves
Gertrude Steinert
Tegeste Stewart
Elizabeth Stieglitz
Sister C. D. Stiles
Charlotte Stovall
Judy Strickland
Rita Suber
Carolyn Sullivan
Lyna Sully
Karen Sutton
Dolores Szabolcsi
Jenny Teets
Sister Tefre
Sharon Thacker
Aline Thomas
Helen Thompson
Mary Thompson
Molly Thompson
Regina Thompson
Beverly Tilley
Hilda Tinus
Pauline Tolstad
Paula Townsley
Susan Tracy
Mrs. L. J. Turkington
Elizabeth Turner

Dianna Tuttle
Mrs. Timothy Urshan
Lolita Vacca
Marla Van Beek
Marion Vannoy
Bessie Varnado
Joann Varnell
Ranae Vaughn
Lorraine Verity
Diana Votaw
Ruth Vouga
Shirley Wallace
Esther Wakefield
Linda Walmer
Yvonne Walmer
Bonnie Ward
Beverly Well
Marzia Well
Bobbye J. Wendell
Irene Wheeler
Fritzi Wheeler
Helen White

Margaret White
Grace Wiens
Ginger Wilkerson
Mrs. H. F. Wilkins
Deanne Willhoite
Marlene Willhoite
Alberta Williams
Janice Williams
Lakelie Williams
Barbara Willoughby
Diola Willoughby
Joyce Wilt
Sister Wine
Deborah Wolfram
Patsy Wood
Beverly Wootten
Mary Lou Wright
Grace Yadon
Sharon Yadon
Joan Young
Mrs. Norman Zeno

Thanks to Virginia Rigdon of the Historical Center of the United Pentecostal Church International and Dorsey Burk of the Foreign Missions Division for their help in researching these names.